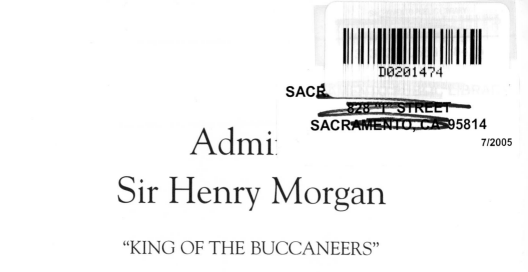

Admiral Sir Henry Morgan

"KING OF THE BUCCANEERS"

Terry Breverton

PELICAN PUBLISHING COMPANY
Gretna 2005

For my family

The word "Pelican" and the depiction of a pelican are
trademarks of Pelican Publishing Company, Inc., and are
registered in the U.S. Patent and Trademark Office.

ISBN 9781589802773

Printed in the United States of America

Published by Pelican Publishing Company, Inc.
1000 Burmaster Street, Gretna, Louisiana 70053

CONTENTS

ADMIRAL SIR HENRY MORGAN: KING OF THE BUCCANEERS

HENRY MORGAN (1635-1688)

'THE SWORD OF ENGLAND'

'THE GREATEST OF ALL THE BRETHREN OF THE COAST'

'The most famous and successful of all the buccaneers was a Welshman, Henry Morgan'
– Frank Sherry 'Raiders and Rebels – the Golden Age of Piracy' (William Morrow & Co. Inc. 1986)

'Ho! Henry Morgan sails today
To harry the Spanish Main.
What a pretty bill for the Dons to pay,
Ere he comes back again.

Him cheat him friend of him last guinea
Him kill both friar and priest – O dear !
Him cut de t'roat of piccaninny,
Bloody, bloody buccaneer !'

– old West Indian ballad

INTRODUCTION

The small country of Wales has much to be proud of. Although bordering England, the native Britons of Wales have kept their own language alive for over 1500 years. The country had its 'Age of the Saints' when the Dark Ages spread all over Europe, and Wales was the only Christian country in this period. It is still fiercely independent, and gave England its greatest monarchy, when Henry Tudor established the reign of the Tudors in 1485. This marks the passage of the United Kingdom out of the Middle Ages, and the beginning of the British Empire which eventually sprawled all over the globe. Throughout history it has given the world eminent leaders. The most famous Irishman in the world, St Patrick, was in fact Welsh, as was the legendary King Arthur, Arthur ap Meurig ap Tewdwr. Presidents Thomas Jefferson, John Adams, John Quincy Adams and James Monroe had Welsh blood. Meriwether Lewis was Welsh, as was Daniel Boone. Samuel Adams kick-started the War of Independence with the Boston Tea Party. The Americans Jefferson Davis, John Pierpoint Morgan, D. W. Griffith and Frank Lloyd Wright were proud of their Welsh heritage. Probably the greatest statesman of the 20th century, David Lloyd George, to whom Hitler ascribed Germany losing the First World War, was Welsh. Modern Welsh-Americans include Bette Davis, Nancy Griffith, Esther Williams and Myrna Loy (Williams). In more recent times, Americans will know of Dylan Thomas, Mary Quant, Laura Ashley, Richard Burton, Tom Jones, Anthony Hopkins and Catherine Zeta Jones – all born in Wales, and Welsh through and through.

However, Wales also has its anti-heroes. America's Public Enemy Number One was the architect of the St Bartholomew's Day Massacre. Murray the Hump, or Murray the Camel, was in fact Llewellyn Morris Humphries, whose Welsh-speaking and God-fearing parents had emigrated from mid-Wales. And when we look back at the Golden Age of piracy and buccaneering, by far the two most famous men in the world were Welsh. The most famous pirate of all was Black Bart Roberts, who took over 400 ships in just three years, and almost stopped transatlantic shipping. Forget Blackbeard and Captain Kidd – they captured a handful of ships between them. Roberts was *the last and most lethal pirate.*' (See this author's '*Black Bart Roberts*') And unusually, amongst all the differing nationalities who roamed the seas, the most famous and successful buccaneer, or privateer[1], was also Welsh. This was Henry Morgan, allegedly a barbarous ruffian, who despite these charges, was knighted, made an admiral and became Governor of Jamaica. His is an amazing story – a man who came to the West Indies with nothing, and single-handedly organised constant warfare against the Spanish in the Caribbean and Central and South America. His success, like that of Roberts, is unparalleled in history, but his name has always been unfairly blackened, and associated with infamy.

George Wycherley wrote '*Buccaneers of the Pacific*' in 1924, praising the valiant exploits of buccaneers such as Drake, Dampier, Sharpe and Cooke. However, the Welsh Sir Henry Morgan, Governor of Jamaica, was called a '*murderous monster*', a '*depraved, vicious, treacherous, almost unparalleled human brute, who was born of respectable people in Wales but deliberately chose the most evil life in his vicious age*'. He was involved in '*shocking scenes of cruelty, torture, rape, murder, arson and every conceivable deviltry (sic) that he and his fellow-fiends could devise*'. Thus Morgan was on a par with Pol Pot, Stalin and Hitler. Wycherley took all his facts from Esquemeling, a disaffected Dutchman who sailed under Morgan, and who wrote of the events to please the enemies of Britain in Holland, France and Spain. As Rogozinski notes in his '*Dictionary of Pirates*', '*Morgan is perhaps the best-known pirate, thanks to the Dutch author Exquemelin, who vividly describes his raids. Exquemelin disliked his "admiral" although he respected his accomplishments. By exaggerating Morgan's villainy, he actually increased his fame.*'

However, the Rev. J. Leoline Phillips (*The Historical Sketches of Glamorgan*, 1912) states that '*in comparison with such monsters of wickedness as some other pirates of the Spanish seaboard – for instance the Frenchman L'Olonnais, or Bartholomew Portugues – Morgan was a saint.*'

Even today, distinguished authors do not bother with original sources but rely upon past propaganda for their facts. Hugh Thomas, in his 1997 'The Slave Trade' calls '*Sir Henry Morgan – the one-time brutal pirate, who, by an appointment as curious as it was scandalous, had become Lieutenant-Governor of Jamaica...*' Morgan was never a pirate, there is no proven evidence of any brutality on his part, and if he had not controlled Jamaica, it is unlikely that it would have stayed in English hands. Morgan was in fact the perfect choice to effectively govern Jamaica, surrounded by a host of Spanish possessions. He, alone, had the strength of character and charisma to lead fiercely independent French, Dutch and British privateers in unending attacks upon vastly superior Spanish forces.

We must remember that Morgan was followed by men of all nationalities, whose survival depended upon what they could gain from privateering. Without capturing any enemy ships, there was no income, as in the traditional phrase, *'no purchase, no pay.'*[2] It would have been impossible for him to have total control over his sailors, marines and soldiers in action. Also these were times before the niceties of the Geneva Convention. The Spanish deliberately blackened Morgan's name in the attempt to get him hauled back to London and imprisoned, as their empire in the New World – California, Texas, Florida, nearly all the West Indies, Central and South America (except Portuguese Brazil) became increasingly difficult to control from Madrid. Esquemeling hated Morgan, as he thought that he deserved more of a share-out from the attack on Panama.

This book will show, that as well as being the most famous buccaneer of all time, Harry Morgan organized and led a dozen successful campaigns against massive odds, fighting the greatest military and naval power in the world. Morgan was a superb tactician and strategist of military tactics, and deserves to take his place alongside Sir Francis Drake and the Duke of Wellington in the panoply of history's greatest heroes.

Footnotes

1. The difference between a privateer/buccaneer and a pirate was that a privateer was issued with a 'letter of marque' or commission to fight against a nation's enemy, complementing the navy's efforts. A pirate would attack any nation's ships or ports.

2. *Purchase* meant a prize ship taken at sea, or any loot captured at any ports or elsewhere in the Spanish Main.

ADMIRAL SIR HENRY MORGAN

THE GREATEST BUCCANEER OF THEM ALL

CHAPTER I

THE EARLY YEARS

Henry was the eldest son of Robert Morgan of Llanrhymni[1]. (Llanrhymney or Llanrumney are the Anglicised versions). This village was formerly in Monmouthshire, but is now on the outskirts of Cardiff, with the tidal river Rhymni (Rhymney) forming an estuary into the Bristol Channel. There is another Llanrhymney near Tredegar in Gwent. Both claim Henry as their son. The manor of Llanrhymney was in the ancient Hundred of Newport, and was the property of the Kemeys family before an heiress married a Morgan in the 16th century. Morgan's appearance in the West Indies is still shrouded in mystery. Even his birth is unclear. Morgans also lived at Pencarn near Newport, a mansion owned by the Morgans of Tredegar, and claimed him as an ancestor. They were descended from the 12th century Owen, son of the Lord of Caerleon. Thomas Morgan of Pencarn was known as *'the warrior'* after commanding English forces overseas in the 1580's and 1590's. Thomas's nephew, Sir Matthew Morgan, was wounded at the Siege of Rouen in 1591. Sir Charles Morgan was a Privy Councillor for Charles I.

And of course, the Morgan family held the great Tredegar House, just on the outskirts of Newport on the road to Cardiff. To make matters more obscure, Morgan called one of his Jamaican plantations Llanrumney and the other Penkarne. He was naturally unhappy about the rumours of his early history, of being an indentured servant, suing the publishers of Esquemeling's book on buccaneers. This was the first recorded successful libel action in history. After the successful action in 1684, the English publishers had to add this rider to future editions: *'John Esquemeling hath mistaken the Origin of Sir Henry Morgan, for he was a Gentleman's Son of good Quality, in the County of Monmouth, and was never a Servant unto anybody in his life, unless unto his Majesty, the late King of England.'* One of Henry's uncles was Lieutenant-Colonel Edward

Llanrumney Hall

Morgan[2], noted above, and another was Thomas Morgan, second-in-command to General Monck, and who became Governor of Jersey.

Most histories record that Morgan went as an indentured servant to Barbados, sailing on May 3rd, 1655, where he served his full seven years, before obtaining his freedom in 1662 and he then moved on to Tortuga before settling in Jamaica. The story prevalent in his lifetime was that he had been captured in Bristol and sold as a servant in Barbados[3]. Esquemeling[4] had a variant of this in that he stated that Morgan had been sold by his parents as a boy to serve as a labourer in Barbados. Morgan certainly was in Barbados before he appears in history in Jamaica. It seems that the huge popularity of Esquemeling's biased book has obscured the facts. There was a 'Henry Morgan' indentured in Bristol to sail to Barbados in 1655, but it was a rather common name in southeast Wales. (Cae-Paen field between Llandaff and Peterston, near Cardiff was owned by a Henry Morgan in 1612). Morgan was almost certainly a junior officer in an expedition sent to the West Indies by Oliver Cromwell under the incompetent General Venables. Yet another tale tells us that he was kidnapped as a boy in Bristol (this was a common occurrence), taken to Barbados and deserted his 'owner' when the Penn-Venables fleet reached there, recruiting for the attack on Hispaniola.

Perhaps we can spend a little time here exploring the circumstances of his birth. J. Anthony Pickford, a Newport man who died tragically young, and had been President of the Oxford University Union Society, wrote '*Between Marsh and Mountain*'. He is very precise about Henry Morgan's parentage: '*The eldest son of Thomas of Machen Plas was another Rowland. Rowland's second son Henry and Henry's son Thomas went to Llanrhymney. (The first Henry had married Catherine Kemeys, the heiress of the manor of Llanrhymney. J.W.) Thomas of Llanrhymney's third son Robert was living in London in 1670. It was Robert's son Henry who became notorious as Sir Henry Morgan the Buccaneer.*' He was born in 1635, the son of Robert Morgan, a yeoman farmer at Llanrhymni, and the family was related to the Morgans of Tredegar House just a few miles east.[5] His father's brother was William Morgan of Llanrhymni Hall, and there are many memorials of the family in the nearby Church of St Mellons[6]. The 'great families' of Glamorgan and Monmouthshire in these times were those of Herbert, Stradling, Matthews and Morgan. As we have seen, the Morgans of Llanrhymni, Pencarne and Tredegar House were all notable families. An uncle of Henry was Captain Thomas Morgan[7] of Llanrhymni, a Parliamentarian hero in the English Civil War. Another uncle, Edward, was a Cavalier Colonel who became Governor of Jamaica, and whose daughter Henry married. Thus all the information disseminated by Esquemeling about Morgan being of humble origins is easily disproved.

HENRY MORGAN'S ARRIVAL IN THE WEST INDIES

Morgan arrived in Barbados upon January 29th, 1655, aged around 20, as an ensign with Cromwell's invasion force. The plan was to take Central America and all its riches from the Spanish, first capturing Cuba or Hispaniola. General Venables sought recruits, and took on 1200 men from St Kitts and Nevis, and another 3500 *'of poor quality'* in Barbados. Barbados at the time was not exactly a law-abiding place, and the master of the fleet's flagship wrote: *'this island is the dunghill whereon*

Morgan as a young man

England doth cast forth its rubbish. Rogues and whores and suchlike people are those, which are generally brought here (i.e. transported from crimes). *A rogue in England will hardly make a cheater here. A bawd* (prostitute) *brought over* (here) *puts on such a demure comportment, a whore if handsome makes a wife for some rich* (tobacco or sugar) *planter.'*

The naval commander was the Welshman Vice-Admiral Penn, whose eldest son founded Pennsylvania (and somewhat treacherously refused the Welsh settlers their promised independent colony.) The expedition of Penn and Venables (which had left in 1654) was meant to capture Hispaniola[8] from the Spanish, and nearly 7000 men landed at Santo Domingo on the south side of the island. Disease and incompetent leadership forced the army to withdraw. It was a complete shambles, with 2000 men dying of sickness, so the fleet moved on to Jamaica. Morgan must have drawn lessons from the fiasco.

The poorly defended Jamaica was instead captured in May, in an otherwise disastrous campaign, and Morgan stayed there. Leslie, the earliest historian of Jamaica, noted soon after Morgan's death that at this time Morgan '*saw the excess and debauchery of his Fellows, and that they became reduced to the lowest shifts by their lavish Expenses on their Arrival (in Jamaica), he, having Vast Designs in View, lived moderate and got together as much money as purchased a Vessel for himself; and having a fine Crew, put to Sea.*' Morgan spent the next few years taking part in successful attacks from the new English base in Jamaica, on Spanish towns in South America and the West Indies. Records show that Morgan was in at least two of the successful attacks on Coro (on Lake Maracaibo, Venezuela), Puerto Caballo and Cumana, led by Sir Christopher Myngs[9], Morgan now being a ship's captain given commissions by Jamaica's new governor. Morgan was to return to sack Maracaibo later in his career.

There was an official 'cessation of hostilities' with Spain from 1658. However, the Spanish still captured British ships in the West Indies, and treated their crews as pirates. Thus it was an '*anything goes*' situation off the Spanish Main and in the Caribbean, whereby the peace did not hold. The privateers of the time pleaded ignorance of any peace between the two countries.

Meanwhile, there was still a problem in wresting Jamaica from the Spanish. Appointed the last Spanish Governor of Jamaica, Don Cristobal Arnalso de Ysassi led strong guerrilla forces in its hilly interior. Two expeditions sailing to help him were met off the north coast by General Doyley's forces, and Don Arnalso was defeated near Ocho Rios in 1657 and at Rio Nuevo in 1658. He held out until 1660, when his Maroon (escaped slave) allies deserted him, and he and the remnants of his forces escaped to Cuba in canoes. Doyley was made Governor in 1661, succeeded by Lord Windsor in 1662. War between the English settlers in Jamaica and the Maroons carried on, with a defeat of English soldiers in 1663.

Footnotes to Chapter 1

1. Llanrhymni Hall is now a pub, named Llanrumney Hall, in the midst of a vast former council estate on the eastern outskirts of Cardiff. It is on the site of an ancient monastery, an Elizabethan manor rebuilt in 1824, and was the ancestral home of a branch of the Morgan family. A fireplace photographed in 1910 (now lost or covered over) had the Morgan coat of arms and the date 1587, the year before the Armada. Thomas Morgan of Llanrhymi Hall married Catherine Herbert of Cogan Pill, and they had eight children. The boys were William, who inherited the hall, then Edward, then Robert, and the daughters were Catherine, Elizabeth, Blanch, Mary and Jane. Robert was Henry Morgan's father. Henry Morgan's sister was Catherine and his brother Thomas started the Llangatog branch of the family. Morgan's uncle Edward is mentioned in the next footnote. In 1952, the Hall and its 700 acres were compulsorily purchased by Cardiff Council to build 3600 council houses. There is a legend that Llywelyn II was buried in a wall there, and that Owain Glyndwr stayed at the monastery.

2. Edward Morgan, like his cousin Thomas, served in the Low Countries in the 30 years War, and was known in Holland as '*Heer van Llanrumni*'. He moved on to serve in Germany, and in Westphalia married Anna Petronilla von Pollnitz, the daughter of the Governor of Lippstadt. Edward was made Captain-General of Charles I's forces in South Wales in the English Civil War, and left his family in Germany, safe at Bamberg. After Charles was executed, Edward made his escape to the Continent to rejoin his family. When Edward, a committed Royalist, was rewarded by Charles II with the governorship of Jamaica, he took his six motherless children there, and one of his three daughters married Henry Morgan. His eldest daughter died en route to Jamaica.

3. '*The Present History of Jamaica*', of 1683, is a code of Jamaican laws. A certain act notes that as many white men as possible should be landed in the West Indies and sold there as slaves. Captains and owners of ships, which landed 50 or more such kidnapped whites, would be free from harbour and shipping duties. The slaves were sold and had to serve at least 3 years, when they could buy their freedom at a fixed price and settle on the island. Probably several thousand whites were kidnapped in ports in Britain for this purpose – to settle the island and make it 'British.' Of course, Jamaica at this time was not recognised as an English possession by the Spanish, who still sporadically attacked it.

4. Esquemeling was one of the first proponents of 'niche marketing', with variants for different nationalities – in the Spanish edition, the Spanish were heroes, and the like in the French edition.

5. The great Morgan family of Tredegar House, outside Newport, is famous in Welsh history. Sir Godfrey Morgan, when a captain in the army and before he was Lord Tredegar, rode a horse named Sir Briggs to win Wales' premier race, in front of thousands at Penllyne castle, outside Cowbridge. Sir Briggs then went on to carry him in the front line of the Crimean War cavalry charges at the Alma, Inkerman and Balaclava. Sir Briggs dies aged 28, and its grateful owner erected a suitable monument in the grounds of Tredegar House.

6. St Mellon's Church is on an ancient site, named after a 3rd century Welsh saint who became the first Bishop of Rouen.

7. Thomas Morgan was known as '*The Warrior*', and was described by Sir Thomas Fairfax to Parliament as '*an expert in sieges.*' He had served Bernard of Saxe-Weimar in the Thirty Years War, but returned upon the outbreak of the Civil War to offer his service to General Fairfax. (Oliver Cromwell himself was of Welsh origin, and signed his early documents as *Cromwell alias Williams*) As a colonel under Fairfax, Morgan took part in the siege of Lathom House in 1644, and in 1645 was appointed Governor of Gloucester and commander-in-chief of the district, taking Chepstow Castle, Monmouth and Hereford from the Royalists. Despite suffering from ague, he shared the same facilities as his troops, and always charged in the vanguard of any assault. In 1646 he smashed Charles I's last army in the field, the forces of Sir Jacob Astley at Stow-on-the-Wold. In 1651, Cromwell sent the diminutive Welshman to Scotland, to serve as General Monck's right-hand man. (Henry Morgan later became the best friend of Monck's son). Major-General Thomas Morgan ruled the Highlands, and put down General Middleton's rebellion at Lough Garry in 1654, ending Highland resistance forever. In 1657, Cromwell chose Morgan to lead the army to assist the French in Flanders against the Dutch. Wounded at the siege of St Venant, he commanded the victory in the Battle of the Dunes, and through his skill as a military engineer captured Dunkirk. The great Cardinal Mazarin, Chief Minister of France, and other distinguished persons sought meetings with '*this famous warrior.*' In 1658, returning to England, Richard Cromwell knighted Morgan and gave him control of the Highlands again. Cromwell was deposed by the major-generals Lambert and Lilburne who wanted a military republic. Only General Monck opposed them. Both sides

courted the most capable soldier in Britain, Thomas Morgan, who joined with Monck (who was to become first Duke of Albemarle). Morgan's coming was *a great accession to Monck's party, and a great encouragement to all then officers and soldiers: for he was esteemed by them to be, next to the general, a person of the best conduct on any then in arms in the three nations, having been nearly 40 years in arms and present in all the greatest battles and sieges in Christendom for a great part of that time.'* He was the greatest cavalry leader in Britain, and Monck's cavalry was his weakest link. With Morgan's support, Monck restored Charles II to the monarchy. King Charles immediately awarded Sir Thomas Morgan a baronetcy. War with Holland broke out in 1665 and Morgan was sent to build defences at Jersey as its governor, and died in 1678. With his two uncles being famous military men, it is small wonder that Henry was so successful as a general.

8. Hispaniola is today's Haiti on its western side and the Dominican Republic on its eastern.

9. Myngs is an absolutely intriguing character, who led Henry Morgan on his first privateering adventures, but is hardly known today. As a result, this potted history is included on a man that Samuel Pepys called *a man of great parts and most excellent tongue among ordinary men.'* For a Royal Naval officer to be actually liked by his men was unheard of for centuries.

He was known as a *'tarpaulin captain'*, the captain of a naval ship in Tudor or Stuart times who had risen by promotion through service, as opposed to those *'appointed'* into post because of royal or political favour. The *'tarpaulin captains'* despised the *'gentleman captains'* for their rough use of crews and general incapacity to handle a ship. Myngs was notable for bringing home less than he was reputed to have plundered. He first comes to our attention in 1653, when as a privateer commanding the *Elizabeth*, he captured and brought in a Dutch convoy of merchant ships and its escort of two warships. He was appointed to the *Marston Moor* in 1655 to suppress a mutiny, and brought the men back to a state of discipline.

In Jamaica, Governor D'Oyley sent Captain Myngs, with a buccaneer force of 300 to terrorise the southern Caribbean, and they devastated Cumana, Puerto Caballo and Coro. He took the first major buccaneering booty back to Port Royal after his raid on Coro, the major Spanish city on Venzuela's Lake Maracaibo. Chasing the inhabitants into the forests, the small force of three hundred men found a cache of pearls, cocoa and gold plate, and twenty-four royal treasure chests. They were each filled with 180kg (400 lbs) of silver coins, worth around a million pounds. The Jamaican authorities found out that he had taken 12,000 pieces of eight for himself, and that the expedition had also plundered six Dutch ships, and Myngs was sent back to England to explain himself. He was soon back in the West Indies, attracting buccaneers to his next two trips, including Henry Morgan. With the restoration of Charles II in 1660, Myngs remained in favour, and was vice-admiral of the White at the 1665 Battle of Lowestoft. Admiral Myngs was killed in the *'Four Days Battle'* in 1666, during the Second Anglo-Dutch War (1665-67). His crew respected him so much that a dozen sailors formed a deputation and asked to be given a fireship to salute his funeral, an extremely dangerous task, so that they could *'do that that shall show our memory of our dead commander and our revenge'*.

CHAPTER II – 1659-1663

SANTIAGO DEL HISPANIOLA 1659

Governor Elias Watts of Tortuga gave a commission to a party of four hundred seamen to sack Santiago in 1659, in exchange for a share of the plunder. They divided themselves up into four parties of a hundred men, with a captain appointed at the head of each. Henry Morgan was one of the captains, who then commandeered a French frigate from Nantes. The ship was so overcrowded, that the privateers took another two smaller boats on the way to Hispaniola, and landed at Puerta de Plata on Palm Sunday.

By Wednesday, hacking through forests, the force had reached their objective, St Jago (Santiago) in the island's centre. Just before dawn they attacked and the Governor offered a ransom of 60,000 pieces of eight to spare his life. For a day the privateers looted the town, and on Thursday started back for the ships with the Governor, their captives, and all the loot they could carry. However, a force of a thousand Spaniards had been assembled and it cut off the buccaneers' retreat. Skirmishing was stopped by the threat to stab the Governor, and the buccaneers repeated their demand for his ransom. They boarded their ships unopposed, but freed all the captives without the ransoms, and all who took part made around three hundred crowns each.

1660

From the taking of Jamaica, Spanish guerrillas had been operating from the hills on Jamaica's north coast, and 500 reinforcements were landed there in 1558. They were led by Don Cristobal Arnoldo y Sassi, the son of a former governor, whose brother was Lieutenant General of Havana. Morgan was regularly involved in expeditions against them, along with privateering under Commodore Christopher Myngs. Port Royal was still called Cagway at this time, an Anglicisation of Caguaya, and a fort was built to protect its huge natural harbour. Every few weeks Myng's fleet took to the seas looking for prizes or raiding Spanish territories. The town of Tolu was ransacked. On another raid, Morgan on his ship distinguished himself as 3 large ships were taken. Captain John Morris, a friend of Morgan's, bought one and renamed it the *Dolphin*. Captain Robert Searle bought the largest, of 60 tons and 8 cannon, and called it the *Cagway*, and Captain Lawrence Prince renamed his 4-cannon ship

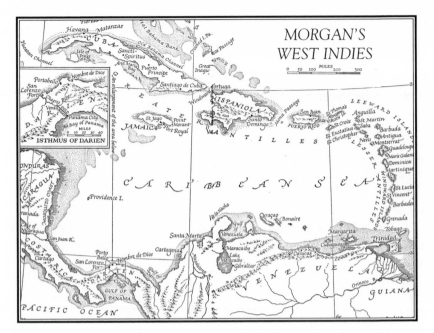

the *Pearl*. From this time, it seems that these four were the most prominent of the Cagway buccaneers after Myngs, with Morgan being their leader. There were around 30 ships operating from Jamaica as privateers at this time, with about 3000 men.

Myngs now took the *Marston Moor* and two other ships, to take Cumana, the capital of Sucre province in Venezuela. Morgan was probably with him, commanding one of the ships. After this, Puerto Caballo, a port in Carabobo province was taken, but without as much treasure as Cumana. Myngs now sailed on to take Coro, the capital of Falcon province, which necessitated a 7-mile overland march through jungle. The privateers captured twenty-two chests, each containing 400 pounds in weight of silver, a fortune worth millions today.

In August 1660, the *Convertine* arrived at Cagway, carrying Morgan's close friend Henry Archbold, with the news that General Monck had restored Charles II to the throne of England, with the assistance of Henry's uncle Thomas Morgan. Monck was created Earl of Albemarle, and peace was concluded with France and Spain, although Charles would not return Jamaica to the Spanish. Colonel D'Oyley was appointed Governor of Jamaica, assisted by a 12-man council. Among those elected were Archbold, and another of Henry Morgan's friends, Thomas Ballard. D'Oyley was ordered to defend Jamaica from any foreign attack, but had no resources except the privateers. In turn, they needed the island to trade their booty. Any help from London would need a ship taking a minimum of 6-8 weeks to reach there, a decision being made, resources gathered, and another 6-8 weeks return journey of any fleet. In effect, Jamaica was always well over three months away from any military support. The unpopular D'Oyley, realising the hopelessness of his task, asked to be relieved and was replaced by Lord Windsor as Governor. Cagway was renamed Port Royal in honour of Charles II, and its fort was renamed Fort Charles, with a new battery of cannon erected alongside it. (Fort Charles is the only one of Jamaica's fortifications to remain intact). Windsor next disbanded the regular army and formed a militia of five regiments. Henry Morgan, fresh from fighting Arnoldo's guerrillas, became an officer in the Port Royal Regiment. Jamaicans kept warning Windsor about the threat from Santiago del Cuba, just 150 miles away, which was supplying the Spanish guerrillas. At the same time, Lord Arlington, of the pro-Spanish faction at court, was made Secretary of State. Things looked bleak for the island.

Windsor had sent the *Griffin* to enquire of Spanish governors in the Caribbean if they would allow trade with Jamaica, and it returned with a curt refusal. His council, because of this *'denial of trade'* decided unanimously that they would *'trade by force or otherwise.'* It was decided to attack the nearby Santiago del Cuba, the second largest port on the island after Havana. Windsor agreed that this would stave off a Spanish attack, and also show the Spanish that the English were serious about keeping Jamaica and free trading in the Caribbean.

SANTIAGO DEL CUBA, CUBA 1660

There was peace between Britain and Spain from 1660, but the Council of Jamaica had decided that it applied only to Europe. In 1662 Jamaica was under threat of attack by the Spanish of Cuba. Upon September 12th, the minutes of the Council proposed *'that men be enlisted for a design by sea with the "Centurion" and other vessels.'* This *'design'* was a buccaneering expedition to destroy St. Jago de Cuba (Santiago del Cuba), the nearest Spanish possession to Jamaica. It was seen as the focal point for the forthcoming Spanish invasion. Jamaica was surrounded by Cuba, Hispaniola, Mexico, Florida (also a Spanish possession) and the Spanish Main of South and Central America. Jamaica was the only British possession, with Barbados, Bermuda, Nevis and part of St Kitts, in this vast area.

Morgan now served again Captain (later Admiral) Myngs, who decided to assault the town and harbour with a fleet of twelve ships and thirteen hundred volunteers. Henry Morgan was commissioned as a captain on his own ship, along with his former privateer colleague Robert

The gun terrace of the Castillo San Miguel at Campeche

Searle on the *Cagway*. The flagships were the *Griffin* and Myng's 46-gun *Centurion*. They sighted the castle of St. Jago on October 5th, but could not sail into the harbour because of the prevailing winds. Another ship, captained by Sir Thomas Whetstone, a debt-ridden Royalist who was a nephew of Oliver Cromwell, joined the fleet. His ship was mainly crewed by Indians, who hated the genocide of the Spanish. Former prisoners of the Spanish told Myngs and his captains that the Castillo del Morro, along with a battery of cannon, and a very narrow entrance to the wide harbour, made a frontal attack impossible. Nevertheless, Myngs was going to follow Windsor's orders until he saw the problems for himself. The Spanish were alerted to his fleet, so Myngs moved away to the mouth of the San Juan River, two miles away by sea, and started disembarking his men.

The buccaneers landed in the dusk, with the men carrying firebrands to see in front of them, to slash through the dense forests. By dawn they had covered just six miles, and were three miles from the fort. After breakfasting, they moved on to surprise the defenders, who had not expected that they could make such quick progress through the jungle. Only two hundred Spaniards, led by Governor Don Pedro de Moralis, defended the town entrance. They were supported by a five hundred-man reserve under Don Christopher de Sasi Arnoldo (-the unfortunate Governor who had lost Jamaica to the English in 1655, and whose brother was still in Jamaica). The buccaneers charged, and the Spanish fled. Six small ships in the harbour were taken.

The privateers (under their letter of marque from Lord Windsor) took the famous citadel, El Morro. They demolished the town and fortress, using 700 casks of captured gunpowder, and the fleet returned with vast booty to Jamaica. Some of the thirty-four guns were taken back to Jamaica, and the others thrown into the ocean. The privateers returned with six prize vessels, silver plate, wine, church bells and hide, to a heroes' welcome, arriving in Port Royal on October 22nd, 1660. Just six buccaneers were killed and twenty went missing. Some had been captured and sent to rot in Seville and Cadiz prisons in Spain, but were released in exchange for Spanish captives in November 1664. Morgan must have been impressed by the ease of the operation, compared to the Jamaica disaster. Lord Windsor now pleaded ill health and returned to England, leaving Lieutenant-Governor Sir Charles Lyttleton temporarily in charge of Jamaica.

CAMPEACHY (CAMPECHE) 1663

Myngs had constantly pressurised Lyttleton to be allowed to attack Spain. Without action, there was no pay for the hundreds of privateers in Jamaica. By Christmas 1662, Lyttleton had weakened in his resolve for peace. There had been no conciliation from the Spanish, and Charles II had sent instruction to Lord Windsor to '*force a trade.*' Besides which, both Charles and the Governor would receive a rich commission if he issued a letter of marque, and booty was looted from the Spanish. There were English log-cutters along the Campeche coast of Mexico, who with great difficulty managed to trade their rich hardwood timber via small ships to Jamaica, and then in larger ships to Europe. Myngs wanted to help them trade, and proposed that the target was San Francisco de Campeche, the capital of the province, know to the English as '*Campeachy.*' It was the most prosperous town on the coastline, built on a Mayan site named Campeche. Myngs thought that, as it had never been attacked, its defences would be weak. However it had a strong garrison of regular Spanish soldiers, guarded by fortresses on two overlooking hills. The Castillo San Miguel was 2 miles to the south, and the Castillo San Jose, 2 miles to the north.

Among the captains given a letter of marque via Myngs were the young Henry Morgan, now aged just 27, and his friends Captain John Morris and Captain Jackman. Sir Thomas Whetstone also joined up. Two famous buccaneers in the fleet were Captain Abraham Blauveldt (who founded the settlement of Bluefields on the Miskito coast of Nicaragua) and Captain Edward Mansveldt, known as Mansfield. Around 14 ships from Port Royal took part, along with four French ships

The walls of Campeche, Mexico

from Tortuga, and three Dutch privateers. With over 20 ships and around 1100 men, Myngs, in the *Centurion*, left harbour in January 1663. They were sent with the blessing of the Council of Jamaica to harry Cuba, Honduras and the Gulf of Campeache.

After sailing a thousand miles, just ninety leagues from Campeache, a huge storm caused one ship to sink and another three to become separated from the fleet. However, on February 9th the remaining ships landed their men a mile or so from the city. Myngs sent a boat to ask the Governor to surrender. The city had a not only regular garrison and the Castillo San Miguel and Castillo San Jose, but also three batteries of cannon between the fortresses, protecting the town and port. Myngs realised that he could not give the Governor long to get prepared to fight and hide valuables, so he launched an attack of buccaneers, armed only with pistols, swords and pikes. Myngs was wounded in three places by gunfire, as his force plundered and demolished what they could, including fourteen ships lying in the harbour. Thirty buccaneers were killed in a whole day of fighting. The stone houses in the town had to be taken one by one, and the grid system of streets made it difficult to move between houses without being shot at. The Spanish counted their losses as 150,000 pieces of eight, and the damage done to the town and forts as costing another 500,000 to repair. Fourteen ships were captured and given crews to return to Port Royal.

Myngs left the Gulf of Campeche with the fleet on February 23rd, but did not return with the *Centurion* to Port Royal until April 13th. The other ships came in a few days later. It appears that the fleet spent some days sharing out and disposing of booty rather than bring it back to Jamaica for the English royal family and assorted ship-owners to take their commission. Morgan now sailed out of Port Royal, flushed with success, leading four other captains, Freeman, Jackman, John Morris and the Dutch David Marteen, and was not to return for almost two years. The original commissions, or letters of marque, granted by Lord Windsor, were still valid. The captains told no one where they were going, and effectively vanished out of Jamaican history from December 1663. They had each made enough from the sacking of Campeche to provision their 5 ships, and perhaps just 200 men, for some time.

CHAPTER III

1664 - VILLAHERMOSA IS TAKEN AND GRAN GRANADA SACKED

1664 saw the first Assembly in Jamaica, passing 45 laws. It was elected by the islanders and consisted of 20 men, meeting in Spanish Town. In 1664, Sir Thomas Modyford arrived in Jamaica as its Governor, bringing 1000 settlers with him. He had been a Barbadian planter and Governor of Barbados. Modyford immediately saw the value of Morgan and his buccaneers, including those who had moved to Port Royal from Tortuga. Their wealth helped his encouragement of agriculture, especially in the cocoa and sugar cane plantations. As Taylor wrote a few years later: (what)*'chiefly advanced its wealth, was the vast sums of Money, and Plate, brought in hither by ye English Privateers; which by their great courage and unheard of Attempts, they took daily from the Spaniards.'* At this time the importation of slaves from Africa increased immensely.

Sir Thomas Modyford was now in place as Governor of Jamaica, and Henry's uncle, Colonel Sir Edward Morgan had been appointed Deputy-Governor, a reward for his Royalist service and support in the English Civil War. His wife had recently died, and his eldest daughter died on the crossing. Bledri Morgan, a distant cousin of Henry's, had come out also around 1662, and acted as one of Henry's lieutenants. The Morgan family was greeted with the news that their kinsman had left the island six months previously, and his whereabouts were unknown. (Henry later married one of Colonel Morgan's daughters, Mary Elizabeth in 1666, and two of his closest friends, Colonel Henry Archbold and Major Robert Byndloss married the remaining two sisters.) Modyford moved the island's capital inland from Port Royal to St Jago, and began trying to convince the settlers to grow sugar on their plantations, as the crop was a success in Barbados.

A letter from Charles II arrived in September, noting the *'violence and depredation'* of Myng's attack on Campeche, asking Modyford to revoke letters of marque to attack Spain. However, Captain Robert Searle with the 10-gun *Pearl* had brought two Spanish prizes in Port Royal harbour and had already landed their cargoes prior to auctioning the ships. Of the captured gold and silver coin, the king would receive a fifteenth share and the Duke of York (as Lord of the Admiralty) a tenth. The Council agreed with Modyford to stop aggression. The ships and booty were to be returned to Cuba, Searle was stripped of his commission, and his sails and rudder were taken off the *Pearl* to ensure his quiescence.

Modyford now had to show the lawless seamen that he meant to stamp his authority on the island. A captain named Munro turned to piracy upon having his commission withdrawn, and took several English ships. Modyford took the ketch *Swallow*, captured him, and hung Munro and his crew in gibbets at Port Royal, at a place later known as Gallows Point. Through influence at court, Modyford now managed to change the remit of London's orders. Privateers, who were out in the Main plundering the Spanish, had to be stripped of their booty and surrender their commissions upon entering Port Royal. He knew that these men would join the French at Tortuga to keep their gains, and that Jamaica would be stripped of its only real defences. His brother-in-law Thomas Kendall wrote of these 1500 or so buccaneers that *'they are desperate people, the greater part having been men-of-war for twenty years.'* Instead, under Modyford's new scheme, they could keep their prizes and prize money, and would be given plantations instead of returning to sea. If they wished to return to sea, they could only attack Dutch Curacao or French Tortuga.

The newly arrived Sir Edward Morgan was given instructions to gather privateers to attack the Dutch possessions of Eustatia and Saba in the Leeward Islands and Curacao and Bonaire off Venezuela. Nine ships joined him, including Captain Searle's *Pearl*, with 500 soldiers and 150 sailors.

1665

Myngs was now recalled with his royal men-of-war to England in 1665 because of the threat of war with Holland. Sir Thomas Modyford, was now forced to rely on privateers from Jamaica, Tortuga and Hispaniola for the defence of the island against Spain. Instead of operating under French letters of marque, these buccaneers now brought their spoils to dispose in Jamaica. King Charles II took a fifteenth of all proceeds, and the Duke of York as Lord High Admiral took a tenth, so the British Crown unofficially approved the privateering.

Sir Edward Morgan's official expedition now sailed to the Dutch West Indies, as the English had declared war on the Dutch. Governor Modyford put the force of 650 men (mainly *'reformed prisoners'* according to Modyford) and ten ships under Colonel Sir Edward Morgan. With over 40 years of active service behind him, Edward made a will, giving his new plantation to his two sons, and a claim on the estate at

Llanrhmyni to his eldest daughter, Mary Elizabeth. He sailed in the 18-gun *Speaker*, owned by fellow-Welshman, Captain Maurice Williams. The smallest ships in his fleet, the *Mayflower* and *Susannah*, only had three cannon between them. Lieutenant-Colonel Thomas Morgan, a distant relative from the great Tredegar House at Newport, was second-in-command. Modyford's plan was that the privateers would destroy the Dutch fleet trading at St Kitts, capture St Eustatius (St Kitts), Saba

One of
Morgans's fleet

(Nevis) and Curacao, and on the homeward leg of the voyage route the French settlements on Hispaniola and Tortuga. Just after the fleet sailed, Admiral De Ruyter with 14 ships attacked shipping at Barbados, and captured 16 British merchant ships at Montserrat and Nevis. Morgan's buccaneers proved troublesome, and had mutinied before their departure from Jamaica, refusing to sail until Morgan promised them

an equal share of the plunder. After three months, the fleet attacked the tiny island of St Eustasius, east of the Virgin Islands, on April 23rd. Thomas Morgan leaped out of a landing boat, ran up the beach towards the 450 defenders in the Dutch fort, and suffered a fatal heart attack. He was sixty years old and extremely corpulent. Thomas Morgan was shot in both legs, but the island was pillaged with very little plunder being found. Colonel Carey took command after the fort was taken and the governor surrendered. There were massive arguments over the sharing of the booty of 900 Negro and Indian slaves, guns, livestock and cotton. Another party of 70 buccaneers crossed over to the island of Saba (Nevis), only 4 leagues away, and secured its surrender also. The fleet returned in some disgrace to Port Royal, as the men were now again in a mutinous state, and could not be trusted to proceed to Curacao.

In July of this year there was news of the fate of Henry Morgan, who had left Jamaica in December 1663. His friend the Dutch Captain David Marteen sailed into Port Royal to give the news, but sailed quickly away to Tortuga when he discovered that Holland and Britain were at war. He said that captains Morgan, Morris, Freeman and Jackman would be arriving soon, having in the past 22 months sacked three great towns, lost all their ships, then captured more ships and were on their way home, with holds stacked with silver and gold. Upon August 20th Colonel Beeston noted in his diary that the captains *'arrived from the taking of the towns of Tobascoe and Villa de Moos in the bay of Mexico, and although there had been peace with the Spaniards not long proclaimed, yet the privateers went in and out, as if there had been an actual war.'* The privateer captains obviously claimed that they knew nothing of the peace, in their immediate meeting with Modyford. They were now rich men, and Modyford took the pragmatic route – he needed them for Jamaica's defence. He wrote to the friendly Duke of Albemarle, who was in charge of overseas possessions, rather than to the pro-Spanish Secretary of State, Lord Arlington, ameliorating the circumstances.

Shortly after this triumphant return, Morgan met his future wife, his cousin Mary Elizabeth Morgan, for the first time. A suntanned and extremely fit 30 year-old, feted across Jamaica, he was wearing faded clothes captured from the Spanish. He was surprised to find that his cousins Charles and another son were clearing his uncle Edward's new plantation, and along with his friends Byndloss and Archbold, discovered the presence of the three daughters of Sir Edward Morgan. Morgan was still unsure at this time if he could keep the gains from his expedition. Governor Modyford was waiting for a favourable answer from London before he could allow the captains to share the spoils. He waited, with his two friends, for the return of Edward Morgan, in order to ask if they could have his permission to court his daughters. However, after a few weeks, it was discovered that Lieutenant-Governor Edward Morgan had died.

Modyford wrote to Arlington of Edward Morgan's death, and the fact that he had died a relatively poor man, asking for assistance for his family. He was still owed money by the king. He also noted the difficulties with Henry Morgan's recent expedition: *'The Spanish prizes have been inventoried and sold, but the privateers plunder them and hide the goods in holes and creeks, so that the present orders little avail the Spaniards but much prejudice his Majesty and His Royal Highness in the tenths and fifteenths.'* He also mentioned that at some time between November 1665 and March 1666, Byndloss, now the commandant of Fort Charles, married Edward Morgan's second daughter Anna. Around this time, Henry Morgan married Mary Elizabeth, the eldest daughter.

Henry was now known universally as Harry, and accepted as the successful leader of Jamaica's buccaneers. Unlike the others, he had friends in high places, so it made sense for the privateers to keep on friendly terms with the Jamaica Council. He took to heavy drinking – he was rich and had a happy marriage, but liked to frequent Port Royal's many taverns with his fellow captains, especially John Morris. David Marteen was tempted back to Jamaica, and also became one of Morgan's crowd.

VILLA DE MOSA, HONDURAS, and GRANADA, NICARAGUA 1665

Henry Morgan had been missing from the invasion fiasco of his uncle. He had been asked to organise Jamaica's militia and defences against the threat of Spanish invasion, and had then sailed in late 1663 on a 22-month voyage. According to Edward Long's 'History of Jamaica', published in 1774, after leaving Jamaica Henry cruised around Cartagena attacking shipping in 1664, and the minutes of the Executive Council of Jamaica show a Captain Thomas Morgan raiding Central America, which must have been Henry. The small fleet of 5 ships and around 200 men had rounded the Yucatan Peninsula to the Gulf of Mexico. Morgan was following Myng's lead in trying to surprise the enemy and chose a town that had never been raided. They carefully followed the treacherous coastline for 150 miles, with its many reefs, small cays, looking for rivers. The fourth river, the Grijalva, could be noted from the change in the colour of the water, and they knew that it was midway between Campeche behind them and Vera Cruz ahead.

Henry Morgan had joined his fellow Welshman, Captain John Morris, and with Captain Jackman they sailed towards the peninsula of Campeache in Central America. Morgan wanted to fortify some islets as a preparation for sending for reinforcements and invading Mexico. However, Jackman and Morris were more short-termist in their thinking. They wanted plunder, and they wanted it immediately. Thus the little fleet sailed south and anchored in the mouth of the River Tabasco on the Gulf of Mexico, and a group of Indians offered to help them fight the hated Spaniards. Just 107 buccaneers landed at Punta Frontera, and entered the village of Frontera, 3 miles inland. Its Indians guided them willingly to Villa de Mosa (Vildemos, Villahermosa), twelve leagues (almost 40 miles) inland. The privateers were expecting to march 50 miles inland to their target, across swamps, streams and dense jungle. They could not take the normal route of a boat upriver, as it was too heavily defended, and without the Indians, the mission would have been impossible. The buccaneers were led on a forced march of 300 miles, avoiding the swamps and all settlements, and according to Modyford's account to Albemarle, easily plundered it, with the element of surprise, and took around 300 prisoners. The town, mainly a trading station for cocoa, was undefended, and the invaders spent their time trying to find worthwhile valuables to plunder. The Spanish had left the town to set up an ambush for the privateers at the mouth of the river. Some 300 Spanish troops were eventually defeated by the better musketry of Morgan's men.

. They returned to their ships, downriver, in boats taken during the sack of Villahermosa. However, in their absence, Spanish ships with 300 crew had taken their five ships. The privateers were fortunate, in that they now captured two small Spanish barques from Vera Cruz and four coastal canoes coming into the river. They sailed and paddled against adverse currents for 500 miles, to return around the Yucatan Peninsula, and carry on raiding the coast of Central America. They then sacked the small fort and market at Rio Garta, near Belize, with just thirty men. The fleet then rounded the Yucatan Peninsula, and crossed the Bay of Honduras. They anchored next off the Isle of Roatan, a large island 30 miles off Honduras, planning an attack on Trujillo, on the mainland. Camping on Ruatan in the Bay Islands, they took on fresh water, and Morgan encouraged some men to stay there as settlers. An English patois is still spoken in Ruatan, where the main village is called Port Royal. Refreshed, Morgan, Morris and Jackman now landed on the mainland to take Trujillo port. Despite being protected by a fort, Morgan took the town and a ship anchored there, and they next sailed 450 miles to the south, to Monkey Point, south of Bluefields in Nicaragua. The voyage had thus far consisted of 2600 miles, the longest buccaneering voyage in the Americas. For over half of it, the canoes had been paddled. Their new ships were of poor quality compared to those they had lost.

They harried the length of the Mosquito Coast, aided by local Indians. Morgan set anchor at the entrance of Nicaragua's San Juan river. Indians told them that there were navigable lakes beyond, with the great city of Granada beyond them. One hundred buccaneers now rowed canoes to capture this fabled city of Gran Granada. They were piloted by Indians, hiding in the islets on the river then on Lake Nicaragua by day, and rowing at night. After five nights and 150 miles from the Caribbean, Morgan was ready to attack this 'impregnable' century-old settlement, with its seven churches and monasteries, and two colleges.

The buccaneers reached the central plaza at dead of night, and overturned the 18 cannon they found there, and quickly took over the barracks and powder magazine. Three hundred dignitaries were herded as prisoners for ransom into the Cathedral. Another 3000 fled. For almost a day the buccaneers looted gold and silver plate, coins and jewels, more than they or their Indian helpers could carry. They sank all the Spanish boats, and were just about to set the Spanish free from the Cathedral before fleeing, when the Indians intervened. They wished to kill all the Spanish prisoners, especially the religious men among them. The pirate captains demurred. They told the Indians that the English did not intend ruling here, and that the Spanish vengeance would be terrible on their tribes, and the Indians reluctantly agreed to let them go. Modyford's official report stated that more than a thousand Indians *'joined the privateers in plundering and would have killed the (Spanish) prisoners, especially the churchmen, imagining the English would keep the place, but finding they would return home requested them to come again, and in the meantime secured themselves in the mountains.'* A few returned with the privateers and were taken on Marteen's ship.

This was a fabulous adventure; little recounted in history books, it rivalled Drake's exploits. It was the most audacious buccaneering adventure ever known in the West Indies. The crews were cheered back into Port Royal, but the captains were called before the Governor. Quizzed by Modyford, two of the captains produced obsolete letters of commission signed by Windsor back in 1662 before Modyford replaced him as Governor. On hearing of the booty, Modyford diplomatically wrote back to London that Central America was *'the properest place'* to attack the Spanish. He gave his immediate approval to another expedition under Edward Mansvelt of Dutch Curacao, supported by Morgan. A soon as he knew of the St Eustatius fiasco, Modyford had persuaded the king to let him send for the reliable Mansvelt, and gave him the title of Admiral of the Brethren of the Coast, asking him to attack the Dutch, with the main target being the wealthy island of Curacao. Modyford had now been allowed to issue Letters of marque, because of continued requests to England from the Council of Jamaica. Previously, Mansvelt had sailed under Portuguese privateering commissions. Mansvelt had already plundered Granada in Nicaragua, and Santo Spirito in Cuba and was the acknowledged *Commander of The Brethren of the Coast.*

CHAPTER IV

1666 SANTA CATALINA, OLD PROVIDENCE

Many years ago, the Dutchman Edward Mansvelt had been elected as 'Admiral' of the Brethren of the Coast, although in reality in Jamaica Morgan had replaced him. Jamaica was still at risk from the Dutch, the Spanish, and the French in Tortuga were trying to lure its privateers away with the offer of Portuguese commissions. Many fine buccaneers had left Jamaica upon their commissions being withdrawn, and Myngs with the real only men-of-war had been recalled to England to fight the Dutch. The Port Royal militia now had 150 members, against 600 previously, and Jamaica's forts were in disrepair, due to lack of funds from London or from privateering raids.

Mansfeld had been asked by Modyford to attack Curacao, as attacking Spanish possessions would cause him too many problems with Lord Arlington. Morgan captained a ship under Admiral Mansvelt, and was made Vice-Admiral because of his attack on Granada. It appears that Morgan had assumed the leadership over Morris and Jackman in Nicaragua. In January 1666, Mansvelt waited in the cays off southern Cuba, for some of the harder types of buccaneer to join him. These men did not trust to land in Port Royal, after the treatment of Searle and Munro. There were no commissions available to attack the riches of Spain, just France and Holland were the targets. Mansvelt then took the fleet of fifteen sail to Curacao, but lingered before pulling away. Perhaps he could not bring himself to attack his own countrymen in the Dutch colony, and instead against orders he took the small Spanish island of Santa Catalina, known as Old Providence, two-thirds of the way from Jamaica to the Isthmus of Panama. (Old Providence is now Vieja Providencia, belonging to Colombia). It appears that Mansvelt now left to try to repeat the exploits of Morgan, Jackman and Morris, once Santa Catalina had been occupied.[1] Morgan went straight back to Jamaica in June, where Governor Modyford congratulated him, and Modyford's brother James was appointed the new Governor of Santa Catalina in 1666.

Mansvelt next returned to Port Royal, but was welcomed with restraint by Modyford, who seemed to accept that Mansvelt was due to be replaced by Morgan in the esteem of the buccaneers. Mansvelt sailed

The West Indies

on to Tortuga, where he suddenly disappeared. Authorities differ whether he was poisoned, or captured by the Spanish and tortured to death. The Spanish from Panama soon retook Santa Catalina, the vital line of communication between Jamaica and the mainland. Its English and French colonists were tortured, and the survivors were sent to work in mines on the Spanish Main. Morgan wrote to merchants and landholders in New England and Virginia, canvassing their support to retake the island. He wanted them to lobby Governor Modyford of Jamaica to give him a roving commission to attack the Spanish. However, Modyford was torn between his desire for a share of the plunder, and the fact that the previous Mansvelt expedition had been an official venture against a warring enemy, despite the fact that he attacked the wrong target and nationality. Poor Modyford's son Jack was imprisoned around this time when the Spanish took the *Griffin* frigate. He was on his way to bring Modyford's wife to Jamaica.

1667

Unlike other privateers, living for the present, Morgan seems to have had a long-term vision of British control of the Caribbean – wherever he went, he wanted to settle. With the retaking of Santa Catalina by Don Juan Perez de Guzman, Governor of Panama, in 1667, Morgan seems to have decided that there were several keys to permanently wresting sovereignty from the Spanish. They were Old Providence (Santa

Catalina), Panama City, Havana, Cartagena, Porto Bello, Maracaibo and Vera Cruz.

W. Adolphe Roberts described the importance of these targets. Old Providence was a small and fertile outpost near the Spanish Main, with plenty of water, which Morgan had already tried to settle. Havana in Cuba was the rendezvous for the galleons of the *'flota'* from all over the Spanish Main, before it returned on the annual voyage of the treasure-ships to Spain. Panama City is still the vital link between the Caribbean and the Pacific. Peruvian gold was taken up the Pacific coast to Panama, where it was unloaded and taken across the Isthmus of Panama by guarded mule-trains, to be shipped from Porto Bello to Seville via Havana. All of Mexico's loot came through Vera Cruz. Colombia and Venezuelan gold was shipped from Cartagena and Maracaibo.

France declared war on Britain in January, and the Treaty of Madrid was signed, declaring peace between England and Spain in May. However, Jamaica was omitted from the document – each country claimed it still. In July, a peace treaty was made with the French and Dutch at Breda, by which Britain gained New Amsterdam (New York and New Jersey). By December, Modyford had the news of all these peace treaties. Jamaica's only real defence was its privateers. Henry Morgan was now commander of the Port Royal militia, and trained them into an effective military unit.

1668

The thirty-three year old Morgan was now elected Admiral-in-Chief of the Confederacy of Buccaneers with the news of Mansvelt's disappearance and probable death. Gosse (1924) made the point that Morgan was *'a brilliant public speaker'*, able to swing opinion of his pirate captains, a skill that served him well against political opponents in later life. Governor Modyford gave him an Admiral's commission in January, at the capital of Jamaica, St Jago, just twelve miles inland from Morgan's usual haunt of Port Royal. (Morgan had also been charged with repairing the island's fortifications and with bringing the Port Royal Volunteers up to 600 armed men, both of which tasks he achieved in 1667-68. Fort Charles was rebuilt)

Immediately, Morgan sought out his Welsh colleague, Captain John Morris. Morgan found two French pirates with information upon Cuba. The pirates had sailed in a sloop from Tortuga, and cruised along forty miles of Cuban coastline. On this unsuccessful voyage, however, they had news of the size and disposition of the Spanish fleet, which was based at St Jago de Cuba (Santiago). The Frenchmen also told him that John

Morris' barque had been sighted returning to Port Royal, after months at sea.

Morris returned with just a few captives and slaves, some rum and sugar, and a few bolts of cloth. The older buccaneer had not had a successful voyage. After unloading, Morgan approached Morris. His men only made about a hundred pieces of eight, with Morris receiving a few hundred, and Morgan taking a commission of another few hundred as Admiral of the Brethren. Morris told Admiral Morgan that he had left a fleet of privateers around the Cuban cays, five Tortuga-French and five English ships in total. Morris also told him of the increasing strength of the Spanish forces in the area around Cuba.

That night in one of the bordellos, Morris is claimed to be the pirate who gave 500 pieces of eight, all his prize money, just to see a prostitute strip naked in front of his drunken men. The going rate at the time to spend a night with a white harlot was around 50 pieces of eight, and twenty for a Negress. If the author may digress here, there is a wonderful Rabelaisian description of this event in W. Adolphe Roberts' 1935 book 'Sir Henry Morgan': 'The barque which had just arrived was of about 100 tons, with a high poop and gunwales scooped to within a few feet of the water. She had sheered up against the beach, and planks were being laid to the serried piles, which served as a dock. Being less ponderous than the boats noted by the observer Richard Blome, she was not forced to unload with 'planks a Float.' Her deck was crowded with men in cotton trousers and ragged shirts, their heads swathed in handkerchiefs that lacked the natty appearance of Morgan's red bandana.... These were the corsairs, among whom - in war attire - it was difficult to distinguish the officers from the crew.

Their prisoners, however, stood out vividly: a couple of livid-faced Spanish officers in rich silk costumes, lashed for pictorial effect with their backs to a mast; but, significantly, no Spaniards of lesser rank. Half a dozen male Negro slaves in chains. Twice that number of young Negresses, stark naked and strutting freely among their new masters. At the sight of the women, a howl of glee went up from the beach. There were shouts to send them ashore first, at which suggestion the followers of John Morris roared in hearty derision.

A diversity of trade goods were brought up from the hold, rushed across the planks and piled on the sand. The haul in this respect had not been important. There were bags of sugar, kegs or rum, bales of leaf tobacco and a few bolts of cloth, for which the usurious Port Royal merchants might be willing to pay 300 pieces of eight, the piece of eight being almost the exact equivalent of our dollar. It was clearly the booty of a single ship, and not treasure galleon at that. The slaves and women, nevertheless, would fetch a pretty price.

Morgan took it all in, chuckling appreciatively. The black wenches filled his eye, and he was glad to see the two Spanish prisoners. Information that he wanted might be screwed out of them, though Modyford was so damned squeamish that physical torture was not to be thought of on Jamaican soil. He had long since made out his friend Morris in the throng, and as chief of the Confederacy he could have gone aboard to talk to him. But Morris was up to his gullet in work, and the High Admiral was contented to wait.

Before the cargo had been half unloaded, the swift tropical night came down like an eclipse. Lanterns were hung along the sides of the barque, and placed here and there on the round, flat tops of the piles… The job was finished at last, and Morris swaggered ashore, the nude Negresses walking behind him, their haunches swinging and their hard breasts puffed out. A squad of men on either side guarded them from the clutching hands of the crowd. At the end of the procession stumbled the male slaves in chains.

It now grew evident why the skipper had made such haste with the unloading, instead of waiting till the next morning. He wanted to cash in immediately the spoils. Competing merchants and brokers rushed up to him, and turned his head unused to figures with their jumbled estimates on this and that. In less than ten minutes, he had accepted a shamefully low figure for the trade goods. Bags of coins were thrust upon him before he could change his mind. He then disposed of the male Negroes at a relatively greater sacrifice, considering their value. But the women he stoutly refused to sell until the following day. Exasperated by an importunate customer, he explained with bellowing curses that he wanted to have some sport with the bitches around the taverns that night before he got rid of them.

Morgan edged through the crowd to his side, and jolted him in the ribs, laughing. "Egad, matelot!" he said, using the traditional buccaneer expression for a comrade. "There is no shortage of strumpets here. White ones to boot! A whole boatload of them have lately come out to us from London".

The other's eyes flashed with delight on seeing Morgan. A few incoherent growls postponed the eternal question of women. He was eager to tell the story of his raid, which, though it had only resulted in the capture of a coasting vessel, would enable him to pay each of his twenty men about 100 pieces of eight, with a few hundred for himself and, of course, a dividend for the Admiral. He had been lucky in finding a casket of money in the enemy commander's cabin. Almost as an afterthought, he added that he had left a fleet of ten buccaneer craft, half English and half French, cruising among the keys south of Cuba. Their captains had sent a message that they would follow Morgan in "any expedition which he chose to plan, so long as it gave promise of plenty of plunder."

The Admiral listened and nodded, keeping his own council, as was his habit. Stalking with Morris up the street towards the taverns, he inquired simply about the Spaniards. Were their fighting ships active? Was there much danger of their coming to attack Port Royal?

Morris replied, blaspheming, that the ocean swarmed with the sails of the pestiferous Dons. But as for their venturing against so strong a place as Port Royal-

"Keep what opinions it may please you to have, yet spread the word that they are sure to be here anon," interrupted Morgan. "I am to see the Governor tonight, and I have a plan. Is there more to be learned from the Spanish officers you brought as captives?" "I flogged them and burned the soles of their feet with hot irons, yet they would not talk," answered Morris in disgust. "So I cut their tongues out." Morgan shrugged.

It would have suited him to go at once to visit Modyford, and to take John Morris along as a witness. Thus to spoil the orgy which John had been planning for weeks was not to be thought of, however. Morgan was not averse to the concession. He enjoyed orgies, despite the fact that he had been married for some years to his cousin Mary Elizabeth, daughter of the late Colonel Edward Morgan, a former Deputy-General of Jamaica.

The mob of buccaneers and their hangers-on growing more vocally riotous every minute, they arrived among the drinking-places and selected the same tavern where Morgan had had his rum in the afternoon. The first act was to divide the prize money - the purchase, as it was called in the current slang of the business - and this was done at a great mahogany table, Morris personally distributing the heaps of coins and receiving no complaints. There would be an additional share when the black wenches had been sold at auction on the morrow.

Shouts of joy resounded after the last man had been paid off. The pirates scattered to the bar and to smaller tables, where they yelled for liquor and immediately began throwing their money around without counting the change. More civilised meals than they ever had been having aboardship were ordered, too. The provender, even so, was limited to huge grilled beefsteaks and bread, with tropical fruit for dessert.

In an hour, the company was both gorged and intoxicated. Their appetites turned towards sex, and they bawled to the Negresses to dance. The latter had eaten heartily, but this did not prevent them from prancing around with energy and shamelessly slapping their buttocks, shaking their breasts, and exploding with jungle laughter. Whenever the fancy struck him, a man would get up, seize one of the cavorting females and drag her into the adjoining passage to be possessed. As the orgy heightened, the nearest open space upon the floor became good enough. Morgan shook with sardonic mirth. The mob of sightseers that jostled in the doorway and stood jammed outside every window looked on enviously....

Abruptly, the pirates tired of the Negresses. They called boisterously for white harlots, and presently a score of these came mincing in from bordellos in an adjoining street. They were dissipated-looking trollops, on whom the climate was telling; but they were dressed in what seemed fashionable and luxurious raiment to the men of the sea. Corseted snugly in high-waisted frocks that were slightly bouffant at the hips, and wearing small satin shoes, they paraded with a semblance of coquetry and conferred a favour when they sat upon knees encased in filthy, bloodstained cotton.

In the general outburst of enthusiasm, John Morris outdid his companions. He pounded upon the table and roared approvingly. He had evidently been nursing a secret nostalgia for white women. The men demanded more dancing, and the London strumpets complied giggling. But they had to have music played on a wheezy fiddle, and the only steps they knew were those of a sort of jig, and altogether it was not exciting. Inevitably, some lascivious fellow cried to them to take their clothes off, but this they would not do. They explained it was not a matter of virtue. They were not in the habit of displaying their charms for nothing, or in public places, merely that. They were not Negro slaves.

Morris declared that if they wanted money, they could have it. He scattered largesse on the floor, and his followers imitated him with fistfuls of reales and now and then a golden doubloon. The women gathered up the coins, but showed no disposition to oblige. "You!", the captain trumpeted, signalling out a chubby blonde. "A hundred pieces of eight to see you stripped here!" The girl cackled in absurd embarrassment, and shook her head. "Two hundred pieces of eight - five hundred!" Morris challenged. "Five hundred pieces of eight, for that!" she repeated, wondering. "Aye, God's wounds! I am a man of my word."

She hesitated, and then began to tear off her clothes. Soon she was mother naked, and gaining confidence she flaunted in a wide circle, her thick, pink body marked on the torso with welts made by the ribs of her corset. The buccaneers seethed and howled and foamed at the mouth, in unbridled jubilation at the spectacle. Morris, the most demonstrative of the lot, hammered on the table with both fists and fairly thundered his lustful satisfaction. He drew from his wallet the price agreed upon and paid it with a flourish.

Henry Morgan sat fingering his wisp of moustache and grinning faintly. That was a diverting show, he thought, but what crackpots men were! The greater part of Morris's dividend from the purchase spent just to see a London slut on the tavern floor without her clothes. Why, he could have had her for the rest of the night, striped and bedamned to her behind a locked door, for a tenth of the sum....' (Thus the Welsh can claim to have invented the strip-show!)

Morgan reported the (probably false) news of the invasion fleet to Modyford. The Jamaica Council was convened, and made the natural

"Morgan's buccaneers attack Puerto Principe in 1668".

choice of the charismatic Colonel of the Port Royal Volunteers, the Admiral of the Brethren of the Coast, Henry Morgan, to assemble a fleet of privateers to set out to ascertain Spanish intentions off Cuba. Morris next decided to join Morgan's commission from Modyford, and to meet up with ships off Cuba. Morgan took two of his own barques, and with Morris sailed off to the Cuban cays on March 30. His commission was signed by Modyford, asking Morgan to organise '*the brethren of the coast*' to '*take prisoners of the Spanish nation, whereby you may gain information of that enemy to attack Jamaica, of which I have had frequent and strong advice.*' Harry Morgan was now a plantation owner of note, and had become close to Modyford, becoming a regular visitor at Modyford's residence, the King's House in St Jago.

Peter Earle pointed out the importance of the first two Articles of Association drawn up by Morgan and his captains for the 1668 Expedition:

1. *It's agreed and concluded upon by and between the abovesaid parties that whatsoever gold, silver, pearls, jewels, rings, precious stones, ambergreece and beazee* (bezoar-stone) *or other goods and merchandises which are or shall be within the terme of this voyage <u>taken on shore</u> shall be divided man for man as free plunder.*

2. *It's agreed and concluded what ship or shipps shall be <u>taken at sea</u> within the terme of this voyage, the tenths and fifteenths being deducted, the fourth part of what goods are in the houlde of such ship or shipps shall be for the respective shipps of this fleet and their owners, and the other three fourths to be equally shared among such shipps company generally…*'

In other words, looking at the phrases underlined by this author, it was far more profitable for Morgan to take booty on land rather than at sea, '*free plunder*', not subject to the commissions of 10% and 15% to the King and Lord of the Admiralty.

Morgan had examined the legal scope of his 1667 commission very carefully. It did not allow attacks on Spanish ships, but did allow him to stop Spanish shipping to determine if the Spanish were plotting against England. It would be easy for him therefore to 'discover' some concocted plot to give him a rationale for aggression. Also, the commission's failure to endorse land attacks made this option extremely attractive, as the booty could thus be shared out amongst the buccaneers, without worrying about giving 50% of the proceeds to the ship owners and the Crown. Each man could make double the money, so Morgan was constantly searching for land targets. Therefore the contract he drew up with the captains and crews distinguished between this 'free plunder' taken on land, and goods captured from ships which would have to be taken back to a Prize Court for distribution by a formula. Thus after every raid, he shared the proceeds, sometimes at Ile des Vaches, before returning to Port Royal.

PUERTO DEL PRINCIPE (now called CAMAGUEY) CUBA 1668

The treaty of peace had been signed at Madrid on 23 May 1667, but the Spanish crown would not recognise British possession of Jamaica. Cromwell's force had only taken the island, more by accident than design, in 1655. In the West Indies Spain still claimed a monopoly of trade, maintained by armed forces. Modyford had asked for a naval frigate to be sent to protect Jamaica, because of reports that a Spanish invasion army and fleet were being assembled in Cuba and Panama. When no response came, he had quickly commissioned Henry Morgan as Admiral in January 1668. At the same time, Beeston's diary refers to Henry as General Morgan.

The privateers off Cuba flocked to serve under a man of Morgan's reputation. By joining up with nine ships, he eventually had a fleet of twelve sail and over 700 men, 450 of whom were English. This seems to have been the time when the writer Esquemeling first sailed under Morgan. A Council of the Brotherhood was held at Twelve League Cays, a coral reef off the Cuban Province of Puerto Principe. Morgan proposed a night attack on the great city of Havana, to cut links between Mexico and Spain. However, ex-prisoners who had escaped from Havana were of the opinion that it needed 1500 men to take the heavily defended port, and even then there was no guarantee of success. Unwillingly, Morgan had to accede to the democratic decision of the council. This was the 'code of the coast'.

A privateer who knew the town of Puerto Principe then swayed the council. Although 50 miles from the sea, it was rich, full of merchants dealing in hides, and not well defended. (It was called Puerto, or port, because the citizens of the port had moved inland years before because of constant buccaneer attacks). Morgan left his ships guarded and hidden amongst the cays off southern Cuba, and set off to trek fifty miles to attack Puerto Principe, said to be the second largest town on the island, and the capital of Camaguay Province. However, a Spanish captive, whom the privateers thought knew no English, had eavesdropped on the council meeting. He jumped into the sea at night, swam to shore and alerted the city. Its citizens immediately began hiding and taking away their valuables, and the mayor gathered a force to defend Puerto Principe.

Around six hundred buccaneers marched through woodland to Puerto Principe, where the mayor (*alcade*) had raised a motley force of 800 soldiers, cavalry, citizens and slaves to defend the town. It seems that Morgan had a premonition of danger, as he took his men away from the road, keeping out of sight and not being seen by scouts. His full force arrived on the plain outside the town, and formed a semi-circular formation to meet the oncoming cavalry. The horsemen were thus assailed by musket fire on almost three sides, and the privateers' tight discipline meant that their line was never broken. After a pitched battle of four hours outside the town, the alcade was killed, and the buccaneers moved in to fight their way through the town. Esquemeling noted:

'The Governor, seeing them come, made a detachment of a troop of horse, which he sent to charge them in the front, thinking to disperse them, and, by putting them to flight, pursue them with his main body. But this design succeeded not as it was intended. For the Pirates marched in very good rank and file, at the sound of their drums and with flying colours. When they came near the horse, they drew into the form of a semi-circle, and thus advanced towards the Spaniards, who charged them like valiant and courageous soldiers for some while. But seeing the Pirates were very dextrous at their arms, and their Governor, with many of their companions, killed, they began to retreat towards the wood. Here they designed to save themselves with more advantage; but, before they could reach it, the greatest part of them were unfortunately killed.'

Upon entering the town, snipers were still shooting at the privateers, so Morgan issued an ultimatum that unless the defenders ceased hostilities, the town would be set alight. The inhabitants were locked in the churches of La Merced and San Francisco, while the buccaneers looked for valuables. For a week, the buccaneers interrogated captives to find where plunder was hidden, and refused to feed the citizens locked in the churches. Pickings were small, between 700 hardened men. Four captives were released to get ransoms, but returned with nothing and asked for a fifteen-day extension. Just then a forage party captured a Negro messenger. Letters showed that the Governor of Santiago was on his way to rescue the Spanish prisoners, and telling the prisoners not to make haste in paying any ransoms. Morgan retreated to Santa Maria Bay, with his booty, and gave the Spanish just one day to find ransoms. With nothing coming in, he then made the pragmatic decision to ask for 500 cattle instead, to be brought to the bay, slaughtered, salted and carried aboard his ships. The desperate inhabitants in the churches agreed. Morgan took six eminent hostages, and the Spanish followed with a great herd of cattle the next day. The animals were slaughtered, butchered and salted quickly to prevent the meat from putrefying in the blazing heat of Santa Maria Bay.

In amongst the carnage, an incident occurred which threatened to turn the expedition into a mutiny. The greatest pleasure a boucanier could get was to suck the warm marrow out of the bones of freshly killed animals, and a Frenchman had put aside a pile of bones for himself. While his back was turned, an English privateer snatched the '*toute chaude*' and started sucking it. A fight ensued, and the participants were ordered to settle it by duelling. While the Frenchman was talking to his seconds, the Englishman plunged a knife into his back, killing him, and a riot ensued. Morgan raced to the gory scene on the beach, and told him that he would take the offender in manacles back to Port Royal, to be later publicly hung there, as there was no time for a court-martial to be held. Morgan was a fluent French speaker, and placated the angry French crews.

The crews then quickly set sail to the Isla de las Vacas (Ile des Vaches, Cow Island), a small cay off southwest Hispaniola. This was Morgan's favoured rendezvous for dividing booty after expeditions, as some of his captains and crews could not return to Port Royal because there was a price on their heads. Treasure and goods came to only around 50,000 pieces of eight in money and goods, making a small reward for each man after three months at sea and fighting the Spaniards. Morgan desperately wanted to take another township, but could not persuade the French to follow him. Fighting had broken out between the English and French on the division of booty. Disappointed, around 200 Frenchmen returned to Tortuga, after again asking Morgan to hand over the '*toute chaude*' robber, and Esquemeling stayed with Morgan's forces.

The former Bishop's Palace in Camaguay (Puerto del Principe) has diocesan records that only date back to Easter 1668, the date of Morgan's raid. The first entry in the 'Record of Baptism of White Children' reads

The capture of Puerto Bello, showing Morgan taking Fort Triana

'The English enemy entered this town at daybreak on the Thursday of Holy Week the 29th of March 1668 and burnt all the records of previous baptisms, and they left on the 1st of April, on the morning of the Resurrection of Our Lord which thus served to liberate us also from our misfortunes. (signed) Francisco Galceran.'

PUERTO BELLO, PANAMA 1668

Most of the Frenchmen in Cuba had returned to join the bloodthirsty L'Olonais at Tortuga, but Morgan convinced his English followers that there would be richer pickings, staying with him, with his new letter of marque. According to Esquemeling, *'Captain Morgan, who always communicated vigour with his words, infused such spirits into his men as were able to put every one of them instantly upon new designs; the being all persuaded by his reasons, that the sole execution of his orders would be a certain means of gaining great riches. This persuasion had such influence upon their minds, that with inimitable courage they all resolved to join him.'* He had returned to Port Royal with 8 ships, compared to the 3 barques that he had sailed to Cuba with. It now seems that Captain Jackman returned from pillaging Campeachy, bringing Morgan's fleet to nine vessels and 500 men in the spring of 1668. Suitably prepared, in May 1668 the privateers sailed out of Port Royal, but neither Modyford nor the captains knew where Morgan was leading them. Morgan wanted no Spanish spies alerting his enemies of his potential targets.

Morgan's daring plan was to attack Puerto Bello, Portobello, the great Panamanian port, and the third largest and strongest city in the New World (after Havana and Cartagena). There were only two ways of sending goods from Panama to Porto Bello, and the overland route of 55 miles could only be used in the summer. The other was by mule train to Venta Cruz, 21 miles from Panama, then by water on the river Chagres to its mouth, 76 miles away. If the river was high, this could be effected in 2 to 3 days, but in low water conditions, 6-12 days were needed.

Winter rain and floods made the overland route impossible.

This was one of the ports where the annual '*flota*' assembled to carry the treasures of the Americas back to Spain, and thus had not one, but two reputedly invincible castles protecting the harbour entrance, with another castle in the city. It was the third most heavily defended port in the West Indies, after Havana and Cartagena. Morgan knew there was no point in trying to sail into the port, where he believed the Jamaican invasion fleet was being prepared, so he decided to attack by surprise. In the last week of June he laid up his fleet, 120 miles west of Puerto Bello, and informed the crews of his target. While the privateers operated under the system of '*no prey, no pay*', there was still a great deal of dissent about attacking the great port, and his French ships, with 250 men, refused and sailed off to Tortuga, leaving him with just 450 buccaneers. He told his small band '*if our number is small, our hearts are great; and the fewer persons we are, the more union, and the better shares we shall have in the spoil!*'

This speech struck such a chord among the Brethren of the Coast, that for generations after seamen used to sing a ballad with the words:'

> '*If few there be amongst us,*
> *Our hearts are very great;*
> *And each will have more plunder,*
> *And each will have more plate.*'

Not far from Puerto Bello, the leading privateer came upon a canoe paddled by six emaciated Englishmen, escaping from building the fortifications of Puerto Bello. They gave information upon the town's defences, and told Morgan of their former condition: '*They were chained to the ground in a dungeon 12 foot by 10, in which were 33 prisoners. They were forced to work in the water from 5 in the morning till 7 at night, and at such a rate that the Spaniards confessed they made one of them do more work than any three Negroes, yet when weak with want of victuals and sleep they were knocked down and beaten with cudgels, and four or five died. Having no clothes, their backs were blistered with the sun, their heads scorched, their necks, shoulders, and hands raw with carrying stones and mortar, their feet chopped, and their legs bruised and battered with the irons, and their corpses were noisome one to another.*'

Morgan's men paddled along the coast in twenty-three canoes, and landed at night at the mouth of the river Guanches, a few miles from Porto Bello. His captains included John Morris, Edward Dempster and Robert Delander, all famous privateers happy to sail under his command. His men included 40 Dutchmen, some French, Italian, Portuguese, mulattoes, Negroes and even a Spaniard. Along the southwest of the town stood the magnificent castle of Santiago de la Gloria, and the smaller castle of San Jeronimo was also in the city. The harbour was fortified on either side, with the Fortress of San Fernando on the south, and on the north the 'impregnable' castle of San Felipe de Sotomayor. Cannons thus defended both sides of the harbour, along with other fortifications and batteries of cannon. Morgan knew that a frontal attack would have been fatal. However, in his articles he had recognised the task ahead – he had promised £20 for the first man entering each fort, £20 for the first man to run up English colours, and £10 for each man who successfully placed a ladder against the walls.

With an English guide who had been a prisoner there[2], they surprised and took a Spanish sentry, and learned that only 130 men were guarding San Jeronimo castle in the city. They bypassed Santiago Castle and reached San Jeronimo's walls at night without being seen. The captured sentry called on the governor to surrender, shouting that the 'Luteranos' had an overwhelming force. Governor Sanchez Ximenez immediately fired a cannon, triggering an immediate buccaneer attack, while the garrison was not fully prepared. Sharpshooters picked off the Spanish as they reloaded their cannon, and Morgan offered safe passage if the garrison surrendered. The governor retorted 'Mas vale morir como soldado honrado que ser ahorcado como un cobarde!' (-'Better to die as an honourable soldier than hung as a coward!') They took Santiago Castle, but needed San Jeronimo desperately as most of the treasure was hidden there.

Morgan later reported to Modyford 'We made our way into the town, and seeing that we could not refresh ourselves in quiet we were enforced to assault the castle, which we took by storm, and found well supplied with ammunition and provisions, only undermanned, being about 130 men, whereof 74 were killed, among whom the Castillano was one. In the dungeon were found eleven English in chains who had been there two years... The Governor of the second castle refusing to permit our ships free entrance into the port, we were forced to attempt the taking of it, which ended in the delivering up of the castle and marching out with the colours flying, and the third castle immediately surrendered to five or six Englishmen.'

Esquemeling's sensationalist account is very different to Morgan's. He recounts that Morgan gathered up monks, friars and nuns from his prisoners, and sent them first up the siege ladders to take the castle of La Gloria, where the alcade and many citizens were sheltering. (This statement was later retracted, in a libel action by Morgan). Other reports say that the surviving Spaniards from the first fort were locked in the powder room and blown up. Morgan's followers had started looting, beginning with the Royal Treasury, after the success of San Jeronimo, but guns from La Gloria opened up on them, so Morgan had to restore order and attack La Gloria. A few men took San Fernando, while San Felipe appears to have kept its forces inside its walls for the fighting. La Gloria may have been taken using nuns and monks, but the buccaneers had heavy casualties. The Alcade (Castillano) had refused to surrender although offered quarter, and it was impossible to take him prisoner, so he was shot. The troops from San Felipe still did not leave the castle, perhaps because Morgan's nine ships were waiting outside the harbour.

Eventually the fleet moved in, and still the guns of San Felipe stayed silent. For fifteen days Morgan's men were said to have raped, pillaged and tortured, as noted by Esquemeling. However, in previous raids on Portobelo in 1668 and Providence Island in 1670, Morgan locked up and guarded female captives, so rape probably did not occur. Esquemeling hated Morgan and deliberately blackened his character. The surgeon Richard Browne, who was present at the attack, wrote in August 1671: '*What was in fight and heat of blood in pursuit of a flying enemy I presume pardonable. As to their women, I know or never heard of any thing offered beyond their wills. Something I know was cruelly executed by Captain Collier in killing a friar in the field after quarter given, but for the Admiral he was noble enough to the vanquished enemy.*' San Felipe was running out of food, and its castellan parleyed with Morgan, while Morgan's men over-ran the citadel. Having surrendered, the castellan of San Felipe realised his supreme dishonour, and begged his captors for a bottle of vitriol. He drank it, and took two days to die in agony.

The fort overlooking the entrance to Portobello Harbour

Great treasure was taken, but the custom-house had little Peruvian bullion for the flota, so Morgan announced that he wanted 100,000 pieces of eight or the town would be destroyed with all its citizens. The temporary governor of Panama, Don Agustin de Bracamonte, came to retrieve the four 'impregnable' castles, with 800 soldiers. (Most accounts state 3000 men, but Bracamonte was emphatic that it was only 800). After an exchange of letters, when Morgan was deeply offended to be called a '*corsair*' or pirate, and answered indignantly, signing the letter '*Portobello, City of the King of England.*' Morgan ambushed his vanguard in a narrow canyon, and he retreated in disarray. The next day the governor offered 100,000 pieces of eight to Morgan if he did not destroy the town or its castles. Esquemeling recorded that the governor was amazed that only 400 men could take Puerto Bello, especially with no cannon, and sent a messenger asking him '*for some small pattern of those arms wherewith he had taken with such violence so great a city.*' Morgan returned a pistol and a few bullets, with the message that he would have them back, within 12 months, in Panama. The governor responded '*that he desired Morgan not to give himself the labour of coming to Panama as he had done to Portobelo for he did certify to him he would not speed so well to Panama as he did to here.*'

Somehow the money was scraped together. Morgan spiked the guns of the forts and left the city and its castles in good condition, in return. Esquemeling claimed that Morgan blew up San Jeronimo castle, but again this was a lie. A few years later Lionel Wafer described it as '*very strong*', and it still exists today. Morgan's men were suffering from fever and foot-rot, so Morgan was anxious to leave before the Spaniards realised that he had few able-bodied men left in his command. The Spanish left in Puerto Bello were indignant that Bracamonte had not attacked Morgan's weakened force. Each day around 20 men were succumbing to fever, and the garrison of the castle was reduced to only 30 or 40 men. It had to be changed every day because of the epidemic raging though the privateers.

The privateers had remained for 31 days, and although Esquemeling tried to blacken his name with reports of rape, Morgan wrote in his report to London that '*We further declare to the world that in all this service we lost 18 men killed and 32 wounded, and kept possession of the place 31 days; and for the better vindication of ourselves against the usual scandals of that enemy, we aver that having several ladies of great quality and other prisoners, they were proffered their liberty to go to the President's camp, but they refused, saying they were now prisoners to a person of quality, who was more tender of their honours than they doubted to find in the President's camp among his rude Panama soldiers, and so voluntarily continued with us till the surrender of the town and castles, when with many thanks and good wishes they repaired to their former homes.*' Covering his back, Governor Modyford added a codicil that Morgan should not have attacked the Spaniards on land, '*having commissions only against their ships.*' Modyford had earlier written to Albemarle, telling him that Jamaica was still in dire peril, and that the Royal Navy had to send two men-of-war to defend it.[3] In February 1668, the Privy Council allowed the 5th rate man-of-war, the 26-gun HMS *Oxford*, to sail to the West Indies, after intense pressure from Albemarle on the King. The ship arrived in October, 2 months after Morgan's return, but Morgan had sailed off again a few days before its arrival, with ten ships and 800 men.

The American poet Edmund C. Stedman wrote of the attack on Puerto Bello:

> *'Oh what a set of Vagabondos*
> *Sons of Neptune, sons of Mars,*
> *Raked from todos otros mundos,*
> *Lascars, Gascons, Portsmouth tars,*
> *Prison mate and dockyard fellow,*
> *Blades to Meg and Molly dear,*
> *Off to capture Porto Bello*
> *Sailed with Morgan the Buccaneer!'*

RETURN TO PORT ROYAL

Morgan had returned to yet another hero's welcome in Port Royal, with nine ships carrying jewels, silks and spices, which had been divided up at Ile des Vaches. There was 250,000 pesos worth of booty, the equivalent of 60% of the value of a year's exports from London to all the plantations. The buccaneers dispersed to spend their gains. Port Royal had never been wealthier, and Porto Bello never recovered its former importance. Each man made about £60 in coin, at at Port Royal, according to a disapproving Esquemeling, *'they passed here some time in all sorts of vices and debauchery, according to their common manner of doing, spending with huge prodigality what others had gained with no small labour and toil.'*

At Town House, in Port Royal, Morgan now convinced Modyford that that he had frightened a large Spanish fleet from attacking Port Royal. After *'dispersing'* their fleet, only then he attacked Puerto Principe. It appears that the Spanish *'invasion'* was a red herring to get Morgan his letter of marque against the Spanish. Between 5 and 10% of the plunder went to Modyford, so he did not pursue the facts too closely. Governor Modyford was using his cut of pirate loot to quietly buy up enough Jamaican land to make him the largest plantation owner there. His payment from the Crown was infrequent or non-existent, and he needed proceeds from Morgan's raids. However, Morgan's activities under the letter of marque seem to have been restricted to reprisals at sea, not on land, as Modyford had addended to Morgan's report, which was to cause problems in his later career. Morgan also informed Modyford that he had evidence from Puerto Principe and from Puerto Bello that the Spanish were gathering men for an invasion of Jamaica.

To satisfy his standing as a man of his word, Morgan asked Modyford for an Admiralty Court to be convened, to fulfil his promise to the French privateers, whom he would need on future expeditions. The English 'toute chaude' robber was duly 'swung off' in public, and his corpse left on the gallows for months after. Morgan had kept his promise to his French comrades. It also appears that at this time Morgan's buccaneers were diverting Spanish resources from Florida, thereby not enabling it to be settled properly by the Spanish. Thus Spanish Florida never joined up with Spanish Texas, and the Spanish never pushed up into the American heartlands of the present USA. Morgan may thus have been instrumental in the eventual English take-over of the southern states of the USA.

Morgan took to Port Royal about 500,000 pieces of eight (£125,000 in those times), 300 slaves and a fortune in gold, silver and jewels. He had been greeted like a king on his arrival. Modyford took his cut, Morgan 5%, the captains around 2000 pieces of eight and the men about 400 pieces of eight. 'Artists' such as surgeons, carpenters and navigators received around 1000 pieces of eight. The injured received, according to the expedition's articles, 1000 pieces of eight for blindness, or for one eye 100 pieces. A lost arm or leg was worth 400-500 pieces of eight. If preferred, one slave equalled 100 pieces of eight in payment. Such was the ingress of Spanish money into Jamaica that the piece of eight was traded normally and equalled about 5 shillings, or a quarter of a pound sterling.

There was wild rejoicing in London on hearing the account of Portobello. It was comparable in boldness to Admiral De Ruyter's attack on the British fleet on the Medway in the previous summer, when he burned several warships and towed the flagship *Royal Charles* back to Holland. With this humiliating defeat following just after the Fire of London and the Great Plague, Charles II needed some good news to placate his people. The pragmatic Charles listened politely to the protests of the Spanish Ambassador but refused to recall Jamaica's Governor, or return Morgan's booty.

Footnotes:

1. The Spanish quickly overwhelmed the small garrison of 32 volunteer soldiers, under Major Samuel Smith, sent to hold Old Providence. In August 1668, Smith and Captain Henry Wasey of the *Concorde* were freed from Havana and came into Port Royal. They were skeletal, and covered with sores, having been chained in a dungeon for twenty months. Three more survivors returned to Jamaica a couple of months later, and the others worked as slaves for the rest of their lives. Seventy-two men had tried to defend the island, among them Sir Thomas Whetstone, the errant nephew of Oliver Cromwell.

2. This Englishman, with others had managed to escape from Old Providence and they told Morgan that Prince Maurice, the brother of the Cavalier General Prince Rupert, was chained with many others in the dungeons of Portobello. Morgan then stated that he thought it his duty to rescue them, helping to make his case stronger for attacking a

Spanish city, when he only had commissions for attacking ships. He wrote to Modyford: '*In the dungeon were found eleven English in chains who had been there for two years; and we were informed that a great man (Maurice) had been carried thence six months before to Lima or Peru, who was formerly brought from Puerto Rico.*' These 11 prisoners were survivors of the Old Providence garrison, and had been tortured and were covered with sores, urine and excrement. Their cell measured 11 feet by 12. It seems that their situation inflamed the buccaneers. Morgan discovered that Whetstone and Smith had surrendered on condition of being shipped back to Jamaica, but the Spanish reneged on their promise. Don Jose Sanchez Ximenez, who was now defending Puerto Bella, had made the promise. Whetstone and Smith had vanished, while the other privateers had died of ill treatment.

3. In this letter, Modyford also disclosed that his son had been a survivor of the wreck of the Griffin, had lived with Indians but had been captured by the Spanish. This information was given by Captain Francisco Martin, who stated that the young man was John (Jack) Modyford, who said he was the son of the Governor of Jamaica.

CHAPTER V

1669 THE *OXFORD* EXPLOSION

There was no Lieutenant-Governor appointed to replace Edward Morgan. Modyford wanted as little interference as possible, as he and Harry Morgan virtually controlled the island. They both were aware that the Spanish were preparing to attack. The only way to contain the threat was to 'retaliate first', whereby the privateers, Modyford, the King and Duke of York all prospered. Morgan's preferred target was the heavily defended Cartagena, the largest port on the mainland, through which was transported all Peru's silver and gold.

Harry Morgan now ignored Modyford's cautious warnings[1], and had assembled his small fleet in October 1668 at Ile des Vaches, his favourite rendezvous. His men had spent their money, and there was no more credit from the grog-shops and taverns, so they *'came clamouring to their Captain to put to sea; for they were reduced to a starving condition.'* His ships had been careened and readied for action, and he told his captains to sail independently to the island as quickly as they could. Sailing independent courses, they were asked to enlist any other privateers that they met en route. By this time Morgan had affected the dress by which he is best known. He wore a wig on formal occasions, much like his king Charles II, but his hair was cut short, and almost perpetually kept under a scarlet bandana. Like Charles, he called for his wig when he lay dying. He carried a plumed hat in his left hand, and wore a vest trimmed with silver, linen pantaloons, thread stockings, and shoes rather than boots. His silk and brocade coat was rarely worn as being too heavy and hot, but he always wore his cutlass, and usually carried a pistol in his belt.

Modyford now sent the former Royal Navy frigate *Oxford*, under Captain Edward Collier, with an increased armoury of 34 guns, to Morgan at the Ile des Vaches. The British Government had sent the *Oxford* to Jamaica specifically to be used as a privateer, to fill the royal coffers, and to keep Spain away from Jamaica. It had been refitted by Modyford for a six-month cruise, and needed to take prizes to pay its 125-man crew, as Modyford had no monies to run the ship. Modyford sent instructions that Collier was to be under Morgan's command, in effect placing a British naval vessel under a freelance privateer on a buccaneering raid against Spain, which was to cause grave diplomatic

A typical Buccaneer, with long musket, hunting dogs and clay pipe, as illustrated in the French edition of Esquemeling's history.

problems in London. A Captain Hackett had sailed the *Oxford* from London, but had run away when he had killed the ship's sailing master, running him through with his sword. Captain Collier was ordered to join up with Morgan, and also to investigate *Le Cerf Volante*, a 36-gun French ship, which was alleged to be a pirate vessel, according to an English captain of a Virginia ship which had arrived in Jamaica.

This French buccaneer had sailed into the Ile des Vaches, wishing to work with Morgan, but the memory of Santa Maria Bay when the French had sailed off to Tortuga, and Morgan's insistence on total command, fouled up the negotiations. Morgan gave the French ship one last chance to join him, but they refused. However, running short of food on the Isle, the French had boarded a passing English merchant-man, taken some stores, and paid for them with fraudulent bills of exchange, drawn on Jamaica and Tortuga, before returning to Ile des Vaches. Captain Collier was delighted to see *Le Cerf Volante* and invited its captain to visit his ship. The Frenchman was startled to see the English captain whose stores he had taken on board the *Oxford*, and was taken with his crew to Port Royal. The Admiralty Court found the French guilty of piracy, and confiscated the 36-gun ship, which was renamed the *Satisfaction*. The *Satisfaction* and *Oxford* rendezvoused again with Morgan at the Ile des Vaches in late December. Morgan now had two powerful ships to lead his fleet against the Spanish.

Straight away, on January 2, 1669, Morgan called a council of war of his captains upon *Oxford*, his new flagship. He discussed the taking of Cartagena, the richest and strongest city of the Spanish Main. He and his captains were sitting around a table on the quarterdeck, when there was a great explosion, killing all the French prisoners. A drunken gunner had shot a musket, which ignited a powder barrel. The *Oxford* sank immediately, at Ile des Vaches (Cow Island), off the southern coast of

Hispaniola. 350 men died, including the all the captains sitting opposite Morgan at the conference table. Morgan was extremely lucky, being on board the quarterdeck at the ship's stern, well away from the powder magazine, so was simply blown off the deck and into the sea. Morgan, John Morris, Collier and surgeon Browne were rescued from the water in the course of the night. There were four captains on the other side of the table, Aylett, Thornbury, Whiting, Bigford and John Morris, the son of John Morris snr. All died. Only Morgan, two captains, the surgeon, two seamen and four cabin boys survived – only 10 of 350 men survived the blast. In the bloody seas, other buccaneers cut the fingers off the floating corpses for their rings.[2]

Richard Browne had sailed with the *Oxford* from England and was the surgeon-general of Morgan's fleet, and recorded the explosion - '*I was eating my dinner with the rest when the mainmasts blew out and fell upon Captains Aylett and Bigford and others and knocked them on the head. I saved myself by getting astride the mizzenmast.*' (Although not kindly disposed towards Morgan, Brown noted his moderation towards prisoners, especially women, which seems to disprove Esquemeling's accusations). Morgan's miraculous reappearance prevented the fleet breaking up. Everyone thought him dead. He decided to blame French prisoners for wrecking the ship, to get the English captains on his side. As there were no French survivors, this appeal to patriotism worked well. Besides, six of the remaining English captains, John Morris, Jeffrey Pennant, Richard Norman, Edward Dempster, Richard Dobson and Adam Brewster, know of Morgan's leadership capabilities from the raid on Puerto Bello.

MARACAIBO and GIBRALTAR, VENEZUELA 1669

Henry's only powerful ship, the 36-gun *Satisfaction*, had been recalled to Jamaica to take part in an action supporting the Campeche log-cutters. Admiral Morgan's new flagship only had 14 guns, but was the largest of his fleet of fifteen sail and 950 men. He unfortunately now had to give up the idea of attacking Cartagena, lacking the firepower and presence of the *Oxford* and *Satisfaction*, and roamed the coasts of Cuba and Hispaniola, raiding on a cut and run basis. After a month or so, the fleet was dispersed. Some ships became unseaworthy. Some French privateers left to go on their '*own account*', which left Morgan with only eight very small ships and 500 men. He bought some provisions off an English merchant ship, and decided to land near Santo Domingo for water and to kill and salt some cattle. There were several skirmishes with Spanish troops while he carried out these actions. Morgan could not return to

Morgan at the Battle of Maracribo

Port Royal without booty, and luckily a French captain, who had attacked Maracaibo with the infamous L'Olonnais and Michel le Basque in 1666, recommended a new attack, three years later. The previous one had succeeded with just 8 ships and 650 pirates. He volunteered to guide the little fleet to Maracaibo in modern Venezuela.

The fleet first landed at Dutch Curacao to take on water, then steered south to the island of Aruba, off Curacao, easily took it from the small garrison, and took on provisions. Unusually, Morgan's fleet set off at night, and approached Maracaibo hoping for the element of surprise. After sailing up the triangular Gulf of Maracaibo, Morgan had to sail up a narrow strait, protected by the islands of Vigilias and Palomas, which had a garrisoned castle. The town was protected by this narrow inlet overlooked by Palomas fort, with which Morgan exchanged cannon fire all day. In a night assault by the privateers, the garrison ran away, leaving 16 cannon, huge stocks of gunpowder, muskets and ammunition. They had left a lit fuse to the gunpowder stores, which Morgan personally ran to, and ground out with his boot. The buccaneers spiked the 16 cannon in the fort, took the powder and weaponry on board, and tried to get his ships into the inlet, but the water was too shallow. They then set off in canoes for the 20-mile journey to attack the fort that guarded the town, but this garrison had also fled. Maracaibo had been abandoned, as mass hysteria had taken over with the approach of 'the conqueror of Puerto Bello'. Just over two years earlier, the gruesome L'Olonnais had invaded the town. Just a few old and sick people remained. According to Esquemeling, anyone captured by forage parties was tortured, by roasting, racks and thumbscrews, to find more loot.

The town and area was ransacked for three weeks, but not enough treasure was found, and according to Morgan he captured about a hundred of the richest families for ransom. Henry at last managed to get his ships over the sand bar in the narrow inlet, and proceeded across Maracaibo Lake (an extension of the Gulf of Venezuela, the seawater lagoon is around 150 miles in length by 60 miles wide) for a hundred miles to attack Gibraltar. This was to be one of Morgan's very few mistakes, not leaving a garrison behind at Palomas fort – perhaps he was afraid of over-weakening his forces. Morgan took around a dozen captives as messengers, as he knew that the Spanish forces were concentrated there, and that Gibraltar would resist. The fleet anchored a few miles off Gibraltar, and a canoe with the prisoners was rowed under a flag of truce to its fort. They were told to tell the mayor that unless he surrendered at once, there would be no quarter from Morgan's men. The alcade (mayor) refused to surrender, and Morgan sailed his fleet just within cannon-shot to test the fort's defences. Here there was a spirited resistance from the fort's cannon, so the fleet veered off.

Morgan had noted that Gibraltar had a forest on one side of it, and that canoes could easily land on its beaches. A French captain, who had sailed with L'Olonnais, led Morgan's men through woods to the landward side of the fort. The Spanish spiked their guns and fled to the hills. Because of the advance notice, there was very little loot to be plundered – it had been hidden. 250 prisoners were rounded up and interrogated. Esquemeling states that one Portuguese merchant was racked to the point where both his arms were broken, then suspended from stakes with a rock weighing 15 stones placed on him, before he said where he had hidden 1000 pieces of eight. However, the man survived, so it seems that once again Esquemeing was embellishing the truth for his readers. Next, a slave volunteered to show Morgan where the treasure was hidden in a ship in one of the rivers that flowed into the lake, so 200 men were sent to take it. Morgan went with the other 250 privateers to capture the Governor of Gibraltar, who was on an island in another river.

TRAPPED! THE BATTLE OF THE BARRA DE MARACAIBO 27 APRIL 1669

However, the governor had taken an excellent defensive position, up a steep hill approachable only by a narrow track. Also, much of the treasure had been moved on from the treasure ship, and some of the valuables taken were swept away with privateers and prisoners in a torrential flood. However, the treasure ship was brought back to complement Morgan's fleet, and other captured ships were added.

Morgan now spent four weeks trying to ransom some important prisoners and the two towns. Only 5000 pieces of eight was taken in ransoms. He was forced to release his prisoners and move on, taking some slaves and four of the most important hostages, as three Spanish men-of-war had arrived outside Lake Maracaibo to blockade him. The great ships waited outside the sand bar at Vigilias and Palomas islands, so Morgan was trapped in the lagoon. Two of the frigates had 36 large and 12 guns, and the other 24 large and 8 small, and they had been sent out from Spain under Don Alonso del Campo with specific orders to exterminate Morgan and his men after the sacking of Puerto Bello. The Spanish had repaired the Palomas fort guarding the harbour and put new troops in it, and waited for Morgan to try and break out from Lake Maracaibo into the Gulf of Venezuela. Morgan the Welshman was trapped.

It was this incident that proved to J. Leoline Phillips (Sir Henry Morgan, Buccaneer, 1912) that Morgan was '*a tactician and strategist of the highest order*'. He first sent his fastest boat to scout the situation. Its captain reported that Palomas fort was repaired, and there were three men-o-war with around 100 guns, with the flagship *Magdalena's* guns trained on the strait entrance. Morgan's '*best*' ship had 14 guns. Esquemeling noted that the privateers were despondent, as '*the forces were very much above those of Captain Morgan.*' Harry Morgan immediately tried to bluff his way out, sending a Spanish prisoner, demanding a huge ransom not to burn Maracaibo and wanting a free passage out into the open seas. He quickly put privateers into Maracaibo Fort to prevent an overland attack by the Spanish. The Spanish admiral, Don Alonso del Campo y Espinosa, in answer offered Morgan an undisputed passage if he gave up all his prisoners and slaves. There were even more ships shortly arriving from nearby Caracas. Otherwise the Spaniard promised to fight him and follow him across the seas, or '*command boats to come from Caracas, wherein I will put troops, and coming to Maracaibo, will cause you utterly to perish, putting you every man to the sword.......... I have with me very good soldiers, who desire nothing more than to revenge on you and your people for the cruelties and base, infamous actions you have committed upon the Spanish nation in America*'. (April 24, 1669).

This was a no-win situation for Morgan. From his experience, the Spanish could not be trusted to keep their word. He did not want to end up like Sir Thomas Whetstone or Prince Maurice, a trophy prisoner rotting in chains. However, the Welshman again offered to compromise, as his men did not want to go home empty-handed, but the proposal was refused, so the buccaneers fell back to doing what they did best, fighting. The negotiations had given him plenty of time to plan, and to convince the other captains to follow his course of action. He gathered his few hundred men in the town's plaza, and asked for *their advice and resolutions on the whole matter.* He asked if they wished to give up all they had purchased for their possible liberty, or would they fight for it. Esquemeling tells us that the response was that *they had rather fight and spill the last drop of blood they had in their veins, than surrender so easily the booty they had gotten with so much danger to their lives.* They trusted Morgan – he had never lost a battle. There was to be no surrender. All the men knew their fate if captured by the Spaniards - exquisite torture and death or a slow death in the galleys or mines. Morgan ordered the buccaneers to prepare a fireship (brulot) from one of the small Spanish ships captured at Gibraltar, and followed it out of the inlet on April 30th. The Cuban fireship was to grapple with and destroy the 40-gun *Magdalena*, Morgan would follow it in the tiny 14-gun *Lilly* and take on the 30-gun *San Luis* and the other privateers would attack the 24-gun *La Marquesa*.

Twelve volunteers manned the fireship, which was made to look like a warship. Slave drums were caulked black to look like cannon, and put into ports specially cut in the side of the ship. Dummy sailors were made out of logs, with hunting caps on their heads and put in position. The English flag flew above this dummy privateer, which was loaded with pitch, tar, sulphur, brimstone, and gunpowder with short fuses. On the decks were palm leaves covered with combustibles. The deck planking had been loosened, so any explosion would hurl burning debris and the palm leaves at the Spanish ships. Three ships of Morgan's fleet also had skeleton crews, one carrying Spanish males and slaves, one female captives and the most precious booty, and one just food, stores and merchandise. Another five ships were full of buccaneers, ready to fight to the death if the fireship was unsuccessful.

On the night of April 30 1669, the buccaneers rode at anchor just inside the inlet, but at dawn on May 1st the small ships headed straight for the tall Spanish galleons. The fireship was allowed to approach close to the Spanish flagship, which expected to blow it out of the water with its first broadside. Just a few yards away, the fuses were lit and the Spanish realised their terrible mistake. The dozen desperate privateers managed to throw grapnels to attach to the fireship against Espinosa's *Magdalena*. The buccaneers escaped in the ship's boat, before the fireship blew up. Rigging ropes were tarred to preserve them against salt water, and the decks were sealed with tar, so soon the *Magdalena* was ablaze, and exploded killing most of her 250-man crew. Espinosa escaped in a rowing boat to the shore. The other large Spanish man-of-war, the *San Luis*, was run ashore by her captain and set on fire, rather than fall into Morgan's hands. It seems that its captain expected Morgan's ship to also be a fireship. *La Marquesa's* captain ordered its cables to be cut, but as the crew tried to set its sails, a rope became caught in a pulley and it drifted helplessly. Morgan captured this remaining 24-gun frigate, *La Marquesa*, and made her his new flagship. His men picked up from the seas dozens of men from the *Magdalena*, to add to the 150 they captured from *La Marquesa*.

Esquemeling's almost contemporary description states: '*The fire ship sailing before the rest fell presently upon the great ship and grappled her; which the Spaniards – too late – perceiving to be a fire ship, they attempted to put her off, but in vain: for the flame seizing her timber and tackling soon consumed all the stern, the fore part sinking into the sea, where she perished. The second Spanish ship perceiving their admiral to burn, escaped towards the castle, where the Spaniards themselves sunk her, choosing to lose their ship rather than fall into the hands of those pirates. The third, having no opportunity to escape, was taken by the pirates.*'

La Marquesa became Morgan's new flagship. Unfortunately, the buccaneers were still trapped inside the inlet and could not get past the withering cannon fire from the fort, through the narrows to reach the Gulf of Venezuela. The fort was fully manned by Spanish desperate for revenge. Morgan put Collier and Morris in charge of besieging the fort, while he interrogated a pilot about how the Spanish had known where he was, and about the disposition of arms and men in Palomas fort. Fourteen guns saved from the shipwreck of the *Nuestro Senora del Carmen*, along with two 18-pounder cannon from the *Magdalena* were also positioned in the fort, and its 16 spiked guns had been drilled out and repaired. The pilot, who was not Spanish, was given his freedom and joined the buccaneers, helping to salvage 15,000 of the 40,000 pieces of eight that sank with the *Magdalena*. More coins were salvaged, fused together as pure silver.

The buccaneers attempted to retake the fort, but lost 30 dead and another 30 were badly wounded. Morgan next returned to threaten Maracaibo with burning, and took a ransom of 20,000 pieces of eight and 500 cattle, salted and loaded on the buccaneers' ships. There was further booty found in the wreck of the Magdalena, including gold doubloons, silver sword-hilts and jewels, probably valued at 150,000 pieces of eight. Morgan now threatened Espinosa that he would kill all his prisoners if he was not allowed to leave the Lake, but Espinosa refused. Morgan had no record of killing prisoners, and Espinosa wanted revenge. Equally, Harry Morgan knew that dead hostages were of no use whatsoever, so applied native cunning to the equation. He had little time, as Spanish reinforcements could arrive any time from Caracas by sea, or overland from Panama. While he formulated his plan of action, he ensured that all the loot was apportioned fairly between the captains and their crews. He did not want to lose any ships with more than their share of treasure, and once all the men had been paid, it was in their interests to ensure that they escaped.

Morgan sent boats and canoes from his ships all day to the shoreline just out of cannon shot from the castle. Espinosa could see the boats full of heavily armed men leaving, and vanishing into the nearby mangrove swamps. On the return he could see just a couple of rowers, as on each return trip the armed buccaneers hid in the bottom of the boats. They counted over 300 men as having landed. The Spanish conferred and believed that there would be a massive attack on the castle in the night, as it appeared that the ships had been left almost empty, and that all the privateers were in the woods around the fort. Espinosa swiftly directed that most of the cannons and artillery be moved to face the landward side of the fort and prepare for battle. That night, Morgan ordered the anchor cables to be cut, and the flotilla drifted quietly out into the open seas on the ebb tide. The alarm was not raised until the little fleet was abreast of the fort, and then the buccaneers piled on every inch of sail, and were out of range before the Spanish had moved their cannon back to the ocean-facing side of the castle. Morgan ordered a seven-gun salute to be fired, to further annoy Espinosa.

Henry next returned his Maracaibo hostages to the fort by canoe, as their ransom had been paid, but kept his prisoners from Gibraltar, as no monies had been received for them. The estimate of the booty was 250,000 pieces of eight, including the value of all the prisoners and slaves. Those white prisoners unransomed were sold into bondage. Battling though Force 12 gales, the fleet returned to great rejoicing in Port Royal on 17 May 1669, but Governor Modyford was not there to welcome them. Although the *Oxford* had been lost, it had been replaced by the Spanish capture, *La Marquesa*. Morgan was taken to St Iago to meet the governor, and found out why no Jamaica Council members had been at Port Royal to welcome him. Morgan explained that he had not been able to raid Cartagena, as his commission laid out, as he did not have enough men, so he sacked Maracaibo and Gibraltar instead. Modyford explained that King Charles would disapprove, as attacking Cartagena was removing a nearby threat of invasion, but there was no excuse for taking the other two cities, so far away. Modyford was relieved that Spain's main warships had been disabled or captured, but told

Morgan that both of them would probably be sent home to explain these actions to the Privy Council.

Modyford could not justify their actions inland, and so revoked the captains' letters of marque. The captains quietly bought plantations with their share of the booty, as the Crown took no action against them, and a state of peace was declared in Jamaica between Britain and Spain. Morgan already had one plantation, and found some more land that had not been claimed, which became his second plantation. This was Danke's Lande, now known as Morgan's Valley, in Clarendon Parish, Jamaica. Captain Edward Collier bought an adjoining plantation, and captains Morris and Prince added to their plantations. Henry Morgan's ingenuity and determination earned Morgan the respect of all the 'Brethren of the Coast', and 'that is Harry Morgan's way' became a popular phrase for any feat of daring.

Footnotes

1. Modyford was indeed worried. Back in England, the court was split between those who favoured 'Harry Morgan's Way' and the pro-Spanish faction, fomented by Sir Thomas Lynch and Lord Arlington. News of Portobelo had made Morgan a hero to the people, and both the Spanish Ambassador and his supporters knew that it would be easier to remove Modyford, the man who signed his commissions to attack the French. Modyford was trying to build up the Jamaican economy, establishing plantations and trade, to a point where it was powerful enough to defend itself. The *George and Samuel* had arrived in London after taking part in the Portobelo raid, and each of its humble 'soldiers' had received 600 ounces of Spanish silver, or about £80, a fortune in those times. Modyford reported factually on events, and as his own son had been taken by the Spanish, who were now using the *Griffin* as a man-of-war, and English prisoners were languishing in Spanish dungeons or working in the slave-mines, it was a difficult debate. Modyford regularly reported seized British ships and Spanish atrocities, and Charles II decided to take no action for the present, although he leaned towards the Spanish position. (His wife was the Spanish Catherine of Braganza, and his brother James was a Catholic).

2. The Haitian Government has given permission to excavate the wreck of the Oxford to an adventure travel firm, Adventure Pointe, from 2004. Divers can purchase packages to join the expedition, and the company says: '*This modern-day treasure hunt is expected to recover cannons, anchors, swords, muskets, untold treasure and other pirate booty. The expedition will utilize the most advanced equipment available, setting out to recover and restore the lost pirate treasure, thus preserving its historical and archaeological significance.*' Shortly after it sank, Morgan on the *Jamaica Merchant* had returned to attempt to salvage it, so it is expected that there is still treasure aboard, as well as cannons.

CHAPTER VI

PORT ROYAL,
'THE SODOM OF THE NEW WORLD'

A month after Morgan's return, Modyford had the bad news he was expecting, that the king was furious and the pro-Spanish faction was in the ascendancy at court. He responded by sending back a full account of all his actions since he had been governor. He even kept the King's fifteenth share of the expedition, £600, 'to be employed in fortifications' as the danger was so great, as he had stripped his privateers of the ability to (legally) defend Jamaica. Unfortunately, the greatest advocate of Jamaican defence, Lord Albermarle, died suddenly at this time, but for the time being the king held off from acting against the governor and his admiral.

Morgan was now the undisputed king of Port Royal, roistering in the taverns with his cronies and supporters. Known as Cagway in Henry Morgan's early days on the island, the original Carib-Spanish name for Port Royal was 'cayagua' (literally, island of water). When Cromwell's force under Penn and Venables took Jamaica in 1655, they thought the name 'cayagua' was that of the entire cay, not just the tip of Palisadoes Point. The new port of Cagway was renamed Port Royal in 1660, on the restoration of Charles II, but was still called Cagway by Morgan and his colleagues for some time after. Because of fear of a Spanish invasion, buccaneers were requested to come from Tortuga to bolster its defences, but after the 1660 peace with Spain, many buccaneers were granted letters of marque to attack shipping. By the early 1670's, Port Royal even rivalled Boston for wealth, with a city of 7000 people. In 1662, such was the amount of silver and gold passing through the port, that the English Government considered setting up a Royal Mint there.

It was 'Pirate heaven' with a huge harbour that could take up to five hundred ships, and at the heart of all the West Indies shipping routes, this was an easy market for pirate plunder. It was a series of sandbars and cays, which formed a peninsula off modern Kingston. The waters were 30 feet deep, just a few yards offshore, allowing for easy anchorage. Buccaneering was unofficially sanctioned by the governors of Jamaica, and the lawyer Francis Hanson of Port Royal wrote in 1683 'The town of Port Royal, being as it were the Store House or Treasury of the West Indies, is *always like a continual Mart or fair where all sorts of choice merchandises are daily imported, not only to furnish the island, but vast quantities are thence again transported to supply the Spaniards, Indians and other Nations, who in exchange return us bars and cakes of gold, wedges and pigs of silver, Pistoles, Pieces of Eight and several other coins of both metals, with store of wrought Plate, jewels, rich pearl necklaces, and of Pearl unsorted or undrilled several bushels......almost every House hath a rich cupboard of Plate, which they carelessly expose, scarce shutting their doors in the night.... In Port Royal there is more plenty of running Cash (proportionately to the number of its inhabitants) than is in London.'*

Morgan's playground was also known for its '*grog shops*', gaming houses and brothels, earning it the nickname of '*the Sodom of the New World*'. In July 1661 alone the Council issued licences for forty new grog shops, taverns and punch houses. Amongst them were the *Black Dog, Blue Anchor, Cat and Fiddle, Cheshire Cheese, Cat and Fiddle, Feathers, Jamaica Arms, Three Crowns, Windmill, Three Tunns, Three Mariners, Sugar Loaf, Sign of the George, Sign of Bacchus, Sin of the Mermaid, The Ship, The Salutation, King's Arms, Jamaica Arms* and *Green Dragon*. Even the street names were familiar, Broad Street, Queen Street, High Street, Lime Street, Honey Lane, Tower Hill, Tower Street and the like. Around this time Governor Modyford[1] was making a fortune in commissions from Henry Morgan and other buccaneers. In 1680, there were over 100 licensed taverns for a population of 3000. Around this time John Starr operated its largest whorehouse, in the official 1680 census maintaining an establishment with 21 '*white women*' and 2 '*black women*'. Port Royal was the largest English or French settlement in the New World outside Boston. By 1690, one in four of its buildings were '*brothels, gaming houses, taverns and grog shops*'.[2] A seventeenth century clergyman returned to England on the same ship as he sailed out on, writing '*This town is the Sodom of the new World and since the majority of its population consists of pirates, cut-throats, whores and some of the vilest persons in the whole of the world, I felt my permanence there was of no use.*' It was heaven for traders, who cheaply bought pirate loot, sold it in London at huge profits, and also profiteered by selling expensive supplies to pirates.

Charles Leslie, in his 1740 '*History of Jamaica*' recorded of pirates, that in Port Royal, '*wine and women drained their wealth to such a degree that in a little time some of them were reduced to beggary. They have been know to spend 2000 - 3000 pieces of eight in one night; and one gave a strumpet 500 to see her naked. They used to buy a pipe of wine, place it in the street, and oblige everyone that passed to drink.*' A pipe is a cask of 105 gallons, or 840 pints of wine. Barre's Tavern was one of the more high-class

and defend the security of the island, but gave him carte blanche to attack anywhere he wished. Admiral Morgan could now not only issue commissions, but also attack inland with impunity, although he was still operating as a *'no purchase, no pay'* privateer.

An extraordinary letter attached to the order asked Admiral Morgan to *'take Santiago de Cuba, to kill all male slaves, to send the women hither to be sold, to treat prisoners as ours have been treated, or rather, as our custom is, to exceed them in civility and humanity, endeavouring to make all people sensible of his (Morgan's) moderation and good nature, and his inaptitude and loathness to spill the blood of man.'* The letter also asked Morgan to *'perform all manner of exploits which may tend to the rpeservation and quiet of this Island.'* This commission appears to have been engineered by Morgan, as not only Thomas Modyford, but Modyford's two sons and also Morgan's brother-in-law Lieutenant-Colonel Robert Byndloss, served on the Council. Morgan wanted to cover his own back, just like Modyford, as he became more diplomatically astute. At the same time, in June, Arlington was sending a letter to Modyford instructing that he should *'absolutely and forthwith abstain and take strict care that no descents (raids) be made... upon any lands or places possessed by the Spaniards to invade or plunder any of them.'* Fortunately for Morgan and Modyford, the 6 to 12-week delay (depending upon weather conditions), in receiving messages 3000 miles away from London, almost always worked in their favour.

On July 2 1670 in Port Royal, the Town Crier had proclaimed the resumption of war with Spain. However, on July 8 in Madrid, peace was declared, although this was not known for months in the West Indies. Morgan was given his new commission on July 22, and he invited privateers to join him from his new flagship *Satisfaction*, the frigate that was formerly *Le Cerf Volante* captured by the *Oxford*. The former commander of the *Oxford*, Morgan's old friend Captain Edward Collier was made vice-admiral. Morgan made his headquarters as usual at Ile des Vaches, while French, English and other privateers flocked to his flag. Apart from the old reliable John Morris, Morgan's distant cousin Bledri Morgan joined him at Bluefields Bay. Around ten ships then sailed on to Ile de Vaches to join up with the more irregular buccaneers of Tortuga and elsewhere. Pardal's sister ship was now captured by Collier, commanding six ships, who had recently sacked two towns on the Spanish Main. Another three privateers captured and ransomed Granada in Nicaragua, and on their return to Port Royal were told by Modyford to join Morgan at Ile des Vaches.

With these nine ships and Morgan's *Satisfaction*, there were another 18 English privateers, the largest vessel being the *Satisfaction* at 120 tons, and the smallest the *Prosperous* at 10 tons. Another seven French ships joined, to which Morgan gave letters of marque, the largest being the 100 ton *Catherine* with 14 guns and 110 men. This formidable buccaneer fleet, of 35 ships, had 1846 men and 239 guns. Captain Thomas Searle wished to join with the *Cagway*, but was apprehended by Modyford when he sailed into Port Royal. One ship in the fleet was to cause Morgan problems. Dr George Holmes owned the *Port Royal*, and had given its captain orders to pick up logwood at Campeche. However, Captain Humphrey Thurston instead increased its number of guns to 12, took on 55 privateers, and joined Morgan's fleet. On his way to join Morgan, he captured a better, Spanish ship, which he renamed the *Thomas*, and gave command of the *Port Royal* to James Delliatt, one of the privateers. This prize should have gone to Port Royal for disposal, but sailed on to Tortuga to meet with Morgan. These events were unknown to Dr Holmes until much later.

On July 5th, Captain Pardal had landed at the western tip of Jamaica and had nailed the following challenge to a tree: '*I, Captain Manoal Rivero Pardal, to the chief of the squadron of privateers in Jamaica. I am he who this year have done that which follows:- I went on shore in Caimanos, and burnt twenty houses, and fought with Captain Ary and took from him a catch laden with provisions and a canoe. And I am he who took Captain Baines, and did carry the prize to Cartagena, and now am arrived to this coast, and have burnt it. And I am come to seek General Morgan, with two ships of twenty guns, and having seen this, I crave he would come out upon the coast and seek me, that he might see the valour of the Spaniards. And because I had no time I did not come to the mouth of Port Royal to speak by word of mouth in the name of my King, whom God preserve. – Dated the fifth of July, 1670.*'

The Welsh Captain John Morris on the *Dolphin*, who had sailed with Morgan back in his early days, caught up with Pardal in his *San Pedro y la Fama*, sheltering from a storm in a bay off south-eastern Cuba. Admiral Morgan's fleet had been scatted by the storm on its way to the normal rendezvous. Pardal sent some men ashore to cut off Morris's retreat, and waited until dawn to attack. However, although outgunned 20 cannon to 10, and outmanned by 120 to 60, Morris attacked first at daybreak. The accuracy of the first broadside made the Spanish privateers abandon their guns, and Pardal's larger ship was grappled and he was fatally shot in the neck in the firefight that followed. Surgeon Richard Browne was present, and wrote that '*so ended that same vapouring captain that so much amazed Jamaica, in burning the houses, robbing some people upon the shore and sent that insolent challenge to Admiral Morgan.*'

The attack on San Lorenzo Fort, on the Chargres River

Morris took the Spanish frigate to supplement Morgan's fleet, and found Pardal's commission to attack English ships in his great cabin. The *Dolphin* itself was a former Spanish prize, only 50 tons, perhaps 50 feet long and with 8 guns, and the second largest ship in Morgan's fleet. Shortly after, Captain Edward Collier captured the 20-gun *Galliardena*, which along with Pardal's *San Pedro* had been attacking the north coast of Jamaica. Her captain signed a statement that troops were being trained in Cartagena and Panama for an assault on Jamaica. Morgan gave the ship to the French Captain Gascoine, as the small Tortuga privateers were overcrowded with Frenchmen who wanted to sail with Morgan. Morgan's reports about enemy intentions were passed on by Modyford to Lord Arlington in London.

Governor Modyford wished Santiago de Cuba to be destroyed because Pardal had sailed from there to threaten Jamaican sovereignty. Morgan saw it as being a difficult harbour to break into, with little prospect of great booty, so roamed the Caribbean, attacking easy Cuban targets but not Santiago. He took foodstuffs on board in preference to plunder. A Spanish ship from Cartagena carrying maize was taken, and wild cattle were smoked in Hispaniola, until by mid-December he was ready for his real mission. In December the admiral called in all his

Today's gun terrace at San Lorenzo Fort

foraging ships, revictualled them all and made ready for battle. He then called a conference on board the *Satisfaction* with all his thirty-seven captains. Until this time no one knew their forthcoming strategy. A 17-man council of war was agreed upon, including Morgan, Bradley. Morris, Collier and two French captains from Tortuga. A Welshman, Captain Richard Powell had escaped from St Iago del Cuba three weeks previously, and Morgan later wrote to Modyford that the place would have been '*almost impossible*' to take. Cartagena, Vera Cruz and Havana were similarly discounted as targets.

The fleet's surgeon, John Browne, wrote to Arlington regarding the importance of Harry Morgan in the forthcoming expedition: '*I think fit further to advise your Honour that Admiral Morgan hath been in the Indies eleven or twelve years, (and) from a private gentleman hath raised himself to now what he is, and I assure your Honour that no man whatever knows better, can outdo or give so clear an account of the Spanish force, strength or commerce... Without Admiral Morgan and his old privateers, things cannot be as successful as expected, for they know every creek, and the Spaniard's mode of fighting, and be a town never so well fortified, and the numbers never so unequal, if money or good plunder be in the case, they either will win it manfully or die courageously.*'

The admiral announced to his captains that they were going to take the treasure city of Panama. It would mean crossing the Isthmus of Panama, 50 miles of jungle, and was thought impregnable by the Spanish, the centre of their Peruvian silver and gold exports. With Morgan's record of continuing success, buccaneers unanimously voted *aye* to the venture. On December 3rd, Morgan sent one of his sloops to Jamaica to Modyford, informing him that he was taking to sea 36 ships and 1800 men, as the Spanish were assembling troops at Panama, Puerto Bello and Cartagena waiting for galleons to attack Jamaica. He did not tell Modyford his destination, but set sail for Old Providence, about 600 miles southwest. Morgan's future problem was to try and justify the target of Panama. Situated on the Pacific, it presented no threat to Jamaica, unlike the other cities considered as more suitable targets. Morgan planned the logistics of the expedition meticulously, raiding Hispaniola for water, rum, fruit and for beef to salt and place in barrels, and sent Collier for grain for bread and biscuits. Captain Collier threatened to burn the small town of Rio de la Hacha, unless he was given 4000 bushels of grain, which was handed over. On his way back to Morgan he also took a Spanish ship filled with grain.

On board the *Satisfaction*, every captain now had to be issued with a commission, and articles of agreement were signed. The Duke of York

SHIP	CAPTAIN	TUNS	GUNS	CREW
Satisfaction frigate	Henry Morgan	120	22	140
Mary frigate	Thomas Harris	50	12	70
May-Flower	Joseph Bradley	70	14	100
Pearle	Lawrence Prince	50	12	70
Civillian	John Erasmus	80	12	75
Dolphin frigate	John Morris	60	10	60
Lily	Richard Norman	50	10	50
Port Royal	James Delliatt	50	12	55
Gift	Thomas Rogers	40	12	60
John of Vaughall	John Pyne	70	6	60
Thomas	Humphrey Thurston	50	8	45
Fortune (1)	Richard Ludbury	40	6	40
Constant Thomas	Coone Leloramell	60	6	40
Fortune (2)	Richard Dobson	25	6	35
Prosperous	Richard Wills	16	4	35
Abraham Oferenda	Richard Taylor	60	4	30
Virgin Queen	John Barnett	50	-	30
Recovery	John Shepherd	18	3	30
William sloop	Thomas Woodriffe	12	-	30
Betty sloop	William Curson	12	-	25
Fortune (3) ketch	Clement Symons	40	4	40
Endeavour (1)	John Harmanson	23	4	35
Bonadventure	Roger Taylor	20	-	23
Prosperous	Patrick Dunbar	10	-	16
Endeavour (2)	Charles Swan	16	2	30
Lambe sloop	Richard Powell	30	4	30
Fortune (4)	John Reekes	16	3	30
Free Gift	Roger Kelly	15	4	40
St Catherine F	Tribetor	100	14	110
Galliardena F	Gascoine	80	10	80
St John F	Diego	80	10	80
St Peter F	Pearse Hantol	80	10	90
Le Diable Volante F	Desnangla	40	6	50
Le Serfe sloop F	Joseph	25	2	40
Le Lyon sloop F	Charles	30	3	40
Le St Marie F	John Linaux	30	4	30
Totals		**1585**	**239**	**1846**

was to receive his normal tenth, and the King his fifteenth. Morgan was to take 1%. Each captain had the shares of 8 men, plus another 8 shares for the use of his ship. Surgeon Browne and the carpenters received enhanced terms. Loss of a leg would entail a payment of 600 pieces of eight, one had was worth 600, and both hands 1800. The loss of an eye was worth 100 pieces of eight.

The *Calendar of State Papers* records the personnel on the 28 English and 8 French ships sailing under Harry Morgan:

A fast ship had earlier arrived at Ile des Vaches, from Modyford, with the announcement of the Peace Treaty of Madrid. Morgan seems to have ignored it. One school of thought is that Modyford sent two packets of instructions. One was to go ahead with the expedition against the Spaniards, and not to open the other envelope giving details of the peace. The ship returned to Jamaca, and was sent out again to find Admiral Morgan. Whatever the circumstances, a mere peace with Spain was not going to stand between Harry Morgan and the treasures of the Isthmus. Harry Morgan always had his '*way*'. Back in London, Sir Thomas Lynch had been appointed by Arlington to replace the deceased Edward Morgan as Lieutenant-Governor, with the intention that he would also shortly replace Morgan's friend Modyford as Governor of Jamaica.

OLD PROVIDENCE 1670

On December 21st, Morgan hove to off the west of Old Providence. According to Esquemeling, it had been converted into a formidable challenge, with a stone castle, Santa Teresa, and two forts, San Jeronimo and San Jose. There were forty-nine guns, but only 190 soldiers. One thousand buccaneers landed, but were met with heavy cannon fire from San Jeronimo. They spent the night shivering in the open in a rainstorm, with no rations, before Morgan sent a flag of truce at dawn asking the governor to surrender. Morgan expected the standard refusal, and was going to return to his ships for more supplies before a fresh assault. Instead, the Governor proposed to surrender, subject to a subterfuge whereby he did not lose face to the Spanish authorities back home in Seville.

Morgan agreed to the stratagem, but stipulated that the first sign of treachery would lead to a '*no prisoners*' massacre. Morgan did not want to lose any of his precious force, all who would be needed for the Panamanian invasion. After a mock battle at the walls of San Jeronimo fort, the rest of the fleet disembarked some more of Morgan's men, to head for Santa Teresa castle. On his way from Santa Jeronimo from Santa

Teresa, the governor was intercepted as planned, and '*captured*' as promised. He then led the buccaneers into Santa Teresa, and yielded his sword and surrendered both forts. All 190 soldiers were spared, and 270 civilians, including 134 slaves were also unharmed. This civilised end to the engagement was a shame to the Spanish on the Main for years after. The prisoners were taken on to Chagres. (They were later given a boat to sail to Porto Bello). There was no torture, and little looting, the main priority being to secure extra provisions, 49 cannon, 1220 muskets and 30,000 pounds of gunpowder that was distributed across the fleet. The island's defences were thrown down and cannon spiked, except for the Castle of Santa Teresa, where Morgan left a small garrison. He still had hopes of settling the island, as before, because it was fertile, had plenty of water and was nearer the mainland than his favoured gathering-point of Ile des Vaches. Morgan argued later that his plan, in taking Panama, was that it was the centre of Spanish power – if it was taken, the peripheries of its empire could easily fall.

Captain Henry Morgan before Panama

CHAGRES CASTLE AND SAN LORENZO FORT 1671

Morgan pondered how best to attack Panama. He could once again take Puerto Bello, and take an overland track to Venta Cruz (Venta de Cruces) and then to Panama, but Puerto Bello had been vastly strengthened and re-garrisoned since he last took it. The alternative Chagres river route also led to Venta Cruz, and there the same jungle track led to Panama. Three Spanish deserters in the privateering fleet (the British and French navies held no monopoly on cruelty to their seamen) had told Morgan that there was a fort, San Lorenzo, on the River Chagres, on the approaches to Panama City. Without its capture, and that of Chagres Castle overlooking it, there could be no progress, so Morgan sent one of his most experienced captains, Captain Joseph Bradley of the *Mayflower*, to take it with three ships (Colonel Bradley's 14-gun *May-Flower*, Captain Norman's 10-gun

Lily and one other) and 470 men. Bradley was made Vice-Admiral for the venture and told to take the fort as quickly as possible. If the fort was taken, the privateers could take boats as far as Venta Cruz, accomplishing over half of the crossing of the Isthmus, before picking up the path to Panama. Anchoring off the mouth of the Chagres, there was intense cannon fire from the fort and castle. Bradley devised a plan to take the castle before the fort, as otherwise he could have been fired on from above.

Bradley knew that the capture was impossible from the sea, so he landed three miles away on December 27th, and hacked for miles through the jungle to reach a clearing opposite the main gate of Chagres Castle. Bradley stared at the earthen bank topped with wooden stakes, followed by a thirty-foot deep dry moat, followed by another palisade, which was between his men and the castle. The only way across the palisades and gully was across a drawbridge, which was raised. The Spanish had a capable and confident Governor, Don Pedro de Lisardo y Ursua, in Chagres Castle, commanding 314 regular soldiers, 75 civilians and dozens of cannon. Its eight '*great guns*' controlled the entry to the river, supported by two batteries of twelve cannon. Chagres Castle stood on top of a mountain overlooking the river, and lower down was San Lorenzo Fort, under the command of Don Francisco de Saludo. The buccaneers had held a council of war, and decided to attack the castle.

It is difficult to understand today, but privateers did not expect a long life – as Black Bart Roberts memorably commented fifty years later, '*a short life, and a merry one*' was what they expected. They were superb marksmen, and had a camaraderie, a '*brotherhood*' of equality where no man was supposed to let anyone else down. Driven on by Bradley, they stormed over the first palisade, into the ditch and up the second bank under withering cannon and small arms fire. In response they aimed accurately at the loopholes in the fort's walls, and hurled grenades and firebombs over the walls. The walls were of timber, filled with earth, to withstand the impact of cannon. However, Bradley's men aimed fire-arrows into the walls, and as the timber burnt, some gaps appeared in the walls as the earth collapsed. Bradley had his legs shot off by cannon fire, and the privateers retreated to regroup before attacking again several times. At length they retired in the dusk, to tend their wounds and prepare for another assault at dawn.

The buccaneers were woken by explosions. They noticed flames coming from the fort. One of their fire arrows had started flames in a thatched roof, which had quickly spread across the fort, and most of Don Pedro's troops were engaged in putting out the spreading fires. Under cover of darkness, the privateers lit the two wooden palisades, which burnt quickly and caused more openings to appear in the walls, as the earth and rocks crumbled beneath the fires. The governor ordered all his cannons into these gaps, but musketeers gradually picked off the soldiers manning them. The pirates again charged, with pikes and cutlasses, eventually taking the Citadel, where Don Pedro de Lisardo bravely refused to surrender and was shot dead. Bradley's 470 men had lost just 30 buccaneers but another 76 were badly wounded. 30 Spaniards, many wounded, were taken prisoner, and 360 killed (many had refused quarter, which usually meant a life of slavery for the soldiers who could not get a ransom). All the Spanish officers died bravely in this bloody engagement.

In dismay, seeing the great castle burning above them, and fearing a two-pronged attack from the castle and the sea, Don Francisco de Saludo and his 300 soldiers vanished overnight from the fort of San Lorenzo, not realising the major casualties that Bradley had sustained. Now the way to Panama was open for Harry Morgan.

Footnotes:

1. Modyford kept himself away from the debauchery in the Governor's residence a few miles inland at St Iago, later to be known as Spanish Town.

2. Rum was the favoured drink at Port Royal and aboard ship. Water was likely to be tainted. Rum was also known variously as 'Barbados Water, Kill-Devil, Demon Water, Nelson's Blood' (later) and 'The Pirates' Drink.' It seems to have been dished out regularly every day upon pirate ships, following the Royal Navy tradition. Rum (often called grog) was plentiful in the Caribbean because it was easily made from sugar cane (saccharum officinarum). It was distilled from the 1640's onwards, so is considered to be the world's oldest distilled spirit. Sugar growers cured sugar in clay pots, and as it crystallised, a brown liquid called molasses drained out of the remaining sucrose. This was recycled by natural fermentation, and then distillation to give a clear liquid, which darkened in wooden casks. The French called it 'tafia', and the English rum-bullion, shortened to rum. (Rum bullion may have meant a 'great tumult'). Later, rumbullion was transferred to another drink. Perhaps the term originated because it was 'rum' (odd) to get precious booty (bullion, or alcohol) out of waste products. Brandy was also easy to get hold of, and beer was carried on boats because it lasted a month or so before it turned vinegary. On the other hand, water was usually taken from a river near a port, or from a polluted river, and was only of any use in cooking. Barrels of water quickly became slimy, and water was simply not potable. Pirates were often drunk because there was little alternative liquid. Fruit juices were added to prevent scurvy.

'Rum', in the sense of 'odd', or 'different' was used as a prefix in much 17th and 18th century slang. A 'rum beak' was a justice of the peace, a 'rum bite' a swindle, a 'rum blower' was a pretty woman, a 'rum bluffer' or 'rum dropper' was an inn-keeper, a 'rum bob' was an apprentice, 'rum booze' was good wine (later an egg 'flip' containing port, egg yolks, sugar and nutmeg), a 'rum bubber' stole tankards from taverns, a 'rum buffer' was a good-looking dog, a 'rum chunk' was a gold or silver tankard, a 'rum clout' or 'rum wiper' was a silk handkerchief, a 'rum cod' was a full purse of money, 'rum cole' was newly minted money, a '*rum cove*' was a clever rogue, a '*rum cull*' was a rich fool, a '*rum doxy*' was a beautiful woman, or a pretty whore, and so on and so on. Other terms pirates would have used are '*rum slum*' for punch, and '*rum quids*' for a great share of booty or captured goods.

Some interesting facts about rum are that 'Rum and Bible' ships carried alcohol and missionaries to the new World as part of the Triangular Trade; American colonists each consumed the equivalent of 4 gallons of rum a year; and the French recipe for Planter's Punch was based on an old slave song:

> *One of sour (lime)*
> *Two of sweet (sugar)*
> *Three of strong (rum)*
> *Four of weak (ice).*

Nelson's body was preserved in a cask of his favourite rum after the Battle of Trafalgar, from when we get the slang '*Nelson's Blood*' for rum, but actually he was placed in a cask or brandy and spirits of wine. '*Captain Morgan*' is the most famous brand of rum, and '*Captain Stratton's Fancy*' is a wonderful poem by John Masefield, about the greatest of all privateers, Captain Henry Morgan and the traditional pirate drink of rum:

> *Oh some are fond of red wine and some are fond of white,*
> *And some are all for dancing by the pale moonlight:*
> *But rum's alone the tipple, and the heart's delight*
> *Of the old bold mate of Captain Morgan*
> *Oh some are fond of Spanish wine, and some are fond of French,*
> *And some'll swallow tay (tea) and stuff fit only for a wench;*
> *But I'm right for Jamaica till I roll beneath the bench*
> *Says the old bold mate of Henry Morgan.*
> *Oh some are for the lily and some are for the rose,*
> *But I am for the sugar cane that in Jamaica grows;*
> *For it's that that makes the bonny drink to warm my copper nose,*
> *Says the old bold mate of Henry Morgan.*
> *Oh some are fond of fiddles, and a song well sung,*
> *And some are all for music for to lilt upon the tongue;*
> *But mouths were made for tankards, and for sucking at the bung,*
> *Says the old bold mate of Henry Morgan.*
> *Oh some are fond of dancing, and some are fond of dice,*
> *And some are all for red lips, and pretty lasses' eyes;*
> *But a right Jamaica puncheon is a finer prize,*
> *Says the old bold mate of Henry Morgan.*
> *Oh some that's good and godly ones, they hold that it's a sin*
> *To troll the jolly bowl around, and let the dollars spin;*
> *But I'm for toleration and for drinking at an in,*
> *Says the old bold mate of Henry Morgan.*
> *Oh some are sad and wretched folk that go in silken suits,*
> *And there's a sort of wicked rogues that live in good reputes;*
> *So I'm for drinking honestly, and dying in my boots,*
> *Says the old bold mate of Henry Morgan.*

Rumbullion is the demon offspring of Rumfustian, described by Burl when Black Bart Robert's crew distilled it at Damana Bay, Hispaniola, in February 1721: '*For that catastrophic brew two huge vats were rowed ashore and filled with molasses, skimmings of overripe fruit, a minimum of water and a liberal splashing of sulphuric acid. The liquid fermented for 8 days while a still was constructed. A complicated system of pipes arranged vertically in a trough of water led from a capacious copper vessel over a fire to a spiral tube under a cooling waterfall that continually dribbled over it. A pewter tankard was set under the spiral and drop by paralytic drop the rumbullion filled it. Only the most foolhardy drank more than one mug.'* Rumfustian was a popular hot pirate drink blended from raw eggs, sugar, sherry, beer and gin. A rummer was a glass for drinking rum cocktails. Pirates usually used pewter mugs or coconut shells as rummers. The *'Rummer Tavern'* in Cardiff referred to the days of piracy in the Bristol Channel.

CHAPTER VII

PANAMA 1671

HENRY MORGAN'S MARCH ON PANAMA - A.G. Prys-Jones 1888-1987

Morgan's curls are matted,
His lips are cracked and dry,
His tawny beard is tangled,
And his plumed hat hangs awry:

But his voice still booms like thunder
Through the foetid jungle glade
As he marches, bold as Lucifer,
Leading his gaunt brigade.

Twelve hundred famished buccaneers
Blistered, bitten and bled,
A stricken mob of men accursed
By the monstrous sun o'erhead:

Twelve hundred starveling scarecrows
Without a crumb to eat,
And not a drink for tortured throats
In that grim, festering heat.

Twelve hundred threadbare musketeers
Rotting in tropic mud
Where the reeking, fevered mangroves
Wreak havoc in their blood:

Twelve hundred febrile wretches,
A legion of the dead:
But Morgan in his blue brocade
Goes striding on ahead.

Twelve hundred tatterdemalions,
The sorriest, maddest crew
That ever the green savannahs saw
When the Spanish bugles blew:

Twelve hundred rattling skeletons
Who sprang to life, and then
Like a wild wave took Panama,
For they were Morgan's men.

Morgan's fleet sailed into Chagres on January 2, 1671. Morgan's *Satisfaction*, Delliatt's *Port Royal*[1] and two other ships, ran ashore onto the uncharted Laja Reef because of the force of the winds, and were pounded to wreckage. The crews survived, and all the supplies were taken off them, however. Morgan's luck still held. However, Bradley was dying from his wounds (his legs had been crushed by a cannon ball), there were weevils in the grain, and maggots in the meat they had brought from New Providence. Major Norman had repaired the castle, for Morgan to leave a garrison there. Morgan told his men to go out foraging for fresh supplies, before they started the next phase of the expedition. Some of the men wore the tattered redcoats of the Penn and Venables Expedition that took Jamaica in 1654, and will have known Morgan from that time.

Using captured slaves, the fort was repaired, and 200 men were left there to guard the fleet under Major Norman. Sir Harry did not wish to repeat the mistakes of Maracaibo. Major Richard Norman was made vice-admiral in place of Bradley, and put in charge of the defensive force. The ships were disposed in battle formation across the mouth of the River Chagres, with another 200 buccaneers left on board and in the castle. Morgan had heard that Don Alfonso del Campo y Espinosa, who had almost been his undoing at Maracaibo, had a fleet in the area. He would not be trapped a second time. Morgan scoured round for Spanish vessels to take his men up the Chagres. The 5 lowest draught ships were mounted with cannon, and with 36 captured canoes, with provisions and ammunition, set off up the river to Panama on January 8. Prisoners said that the river was navigable by such boats for five or six days, up to Venta de Cruz, just a day's march from Panama City.

Unfortunately, unusually low waters, terrible heat, stinging mosquitoes and flies made the journey a nightmare. Not all the buccaneers would fit into the crowded boats, so they walked alongside the river, cutting a path through the rainforest. On the first day, they reached the deserted village of Rio de Dos Brozos, but found no food. On the second day, at the

Morgan's route to Panama

deserted defence post of La Cruz de San Juan Gallego (near Gatun), the flat-bottomed boats ran aground. The cannon were too heavy to take on the canoes, so they were left behind. The boats and cannon were abandoned with a guard of 160 men under Captain Robert Delander. Morgan now had 1200 men left to fight – 30 had died at Chagres, and 200 left to guard the ships, of his original force of 1585 men. On the 3rd day, it was almost impossible to travel through the dense swamps. The canoes took half the privateers to Cedra Bueno, and had to return to pick up the other men. And advance party had been sent ahead by Morgan to scout for a path to Panama, and to look out for Spaniard ambushes.

On the fourth day, a guide was found to lead most of the men overland, and the rest continued upriver, with two canoes well in advance in case there was an ambush. Fourteen miles into their journey, a Spanish force defending the riverbank at Dos Bracas, fled at their approach. The point canoes had returned and indicated that they had expected an ambush here. (This detachment of 250-500 men seems to have been sent by Governor Guzman to retake San Lorenzo. The sight of hundreds of hardened buccaneers coming up the river obviously unnerved them). The privateers had to haul the boats through unforgiving jungle from one stretch of water to another, avoiding rapids, shallows and whirlpools.

An advance party of 100 now used cutlasses to fight a path through the dense riverbank jungle, while 900 men followed carrying provisions. The Spanish had burnt every defence post before them, taking all the provisions with them and destroying any crops. Morgan had ordered the malaria-stricken buccaneers to make the expedition with almost empty packs of provisions, expecting easy foraging along the way, but within three days the men were starving. Two sacks of meal and some sacks of plantains were found in a cache, which Morgan confiscated at pistol point, and distributed among the sickest of the force. Fighting off mosquitoes, lurking alligators, snakes and malaria, the starving pirates resorted to chewing leather and leaves, until on January 14 they found a barn full of maize. Morgan apportioned the food, with the sickest men receiving the most. Apart from suffering from scorpion, insect and snakebites, hundreds had succumbed to malaria and yellow fever. The journey ruined Morgan's health for ever. The buccaneers crammed it into their mouths, knapsacks and pockets, and trudged on. An Indian ambush killed a dozen buccaneers, and Captain Thomas Rogers skirmished with a few Spaniards around this time.

On 15 January, they reached the town of Venta de Cruz (Cruces), which was still burning. General Salado's troops had fired it and retreated. Apart from some stray dogs, there was nothing to eat. The only drink available was some Peruvian wine, which made some buccaneers so sick that they thought it had been poisoned. (Alcohol on an empty stomach has similar effects today! Morgan actually encouraged his men to think that it was poisoned.) Morgan knew it would be difficult to get back to the boats with no provisions, so he had no choice but to press on, his men's *stomachs so fermented as to gnaw their very bowels.* He struggled ahead to Panama on the well-worn jungle path. They were now over halfway there, and the trek became much easier. Mule trains were used on this path by the Spanish to bring the riches from Panama to Venta de Cruz for river transport down to the *'flota'* at Chagres. Guards had slow-burning fuses on their muskets, to fend off the ceaseless attacks from native Indians. On January 16, eight men were killed and ten wounded by poisoned arrows from either side of the path. The Indians had allowed the advance guard to pass, before firing on the main body of Morgan's men. Six Indians were later killed in a clearing. Esquemeling wrote *'here, all on a sudden, three or four thousand arrows were shot at them, without being able to perceive whence they came or who shot them... This multitude of arrows caused a huge alarm among the Pirates, especially because they could not discover the place whence they were discharged.'* Morgan ordered his men to spread out into the woods, where they were less of a target and could see the Indians.

After another two days of constant attacks by Indians and by Spanish scouts, the advance party reached open land. The next day, January 18,

Old Panama's Cathedral Tower where the Spanish sought refuge from Morgan

Morgan could see Panama and beyond it the glittering Pacific Ocean. Cattle grazing on the savannah of Matasnillos were slaughtered, for a great feast in preparation for the attack on their great prize, the richest city in The Americas. Spanish cavalry waited at a discreet distance from the invaders, shouting out '*perros*' (dogs). Morgan set up sentries around low earthen banks and bivouacked for the night. There was still a day's march through the forest to reach the city, and he wanted his men fresh for the assault. Panama was not well defended with fortifications. Morgan had sent out 50 men to try and capture someone to give him an indication of the defences of the city. No one expected it to be attacked. The citizens urged Guzman to meet the '*perros*' outside the town to minimise damage.

However, Don Juan Perez de Guzman, Governor of Panama, made an oath in the Cathedral to die in the defence of the city, and priests and nuns prayed for victory against Morgan's savages. There were 2000 Spanish foot soldiers, some of whom were Negroes and Indian natives, a few hundred cavalry and five field guns to defend the city. Ten days after leaving Chagres, on January 20, the 1200 swashbucklers faced the 2400-strong Spanish army. Morgan decided to attack on January 21, after resting his weary men, and drew up the buccaneers in three groups. There was a vanguard of 300 under Captain John Morris and Colonel Lawrence Prince, a main body of 300 under Morgan on the right and 300 under Collier on the left, and a rearguard of 300 under Colonel Bledri Morgan. Bledri had come with news from Modyford, to join Morgan at Old Providence. Many of Morgan's followers were dressed in the red jerkins of Cromwell's New Model Army – they were veterans of the English

Civil War. Morgan called this lozenge formation his '*tertia*', with narrow gaps between the van, middle and rear sections. Aged just 36 years old, Morgan was about to attack the only city that rivalled Lima for the richest city in the 17th century world. He had just 1200 weakened buccaneers, with little dry powder – most had been soddened in the rainforest - and no artillery. His enemy had been preparing for weeks for his arrival, and Morgan could not risk a head-on attack.

Morgan's Musketeers repulsing the Spanish cavalry at Old Panama

The Spanish were drawn up in a stronger position, with cavalry on each wing, and the guns in front of them. On each flank they also had a herd of wild cattle with herdsmen, who were to be stampeded towards Morgan's little army. Morgan now checked the disposition of the Spanish and with his military intelligence noted that a hill on his left protected the Spanish right flank, but was immediately in front of a ravine, preventing it being quickly reinforced. He thus decided to try to outflank the Spaniards with Collier's men, and to gain the hill. They crept through scrubby bush land, down a deep valley and circled a hill to get within musket shot of the Spanish wing. Morris and Prince's vanguard also advanced into the Spanish cannon and musket fire. Guzman saw the danger on his right, and when Collier's men disappeared out of sight, he ordered a cavalry charge upon Prince's advancing buccaneers. A musket fusillade smashed the first charge apart. In the second, and final charge, the cavalry commander Don Francisco de Haro fell almost into the massed ranks of marksmen. The vanguard was still in its wedge formation, allowing for maximum firepower, and the cavalry had to charge into its front, because it was protected by a hill on one side and a swamp on the other. The outside ranks had knelt to shoot, just as in the English Civil War, then the next rank advanced to fire and so on. With no pikes, this rapid and accurate fire was the only way to have beaten the cavalry charges.

Guzman's infantry were ordered now to stand and fight, but some veterans under de Alcaudete had personally seen the results of the '*rape of Puerto Bello*', and in their blind hatred charged without orders. They were joined by the rest, and pushed past the vanguard of John Morris and Prince to attack the right centre under Morgan. The vanguard's muskets and pistols had discharged, and they were now fighting with cutlasses and daggers. Captain Collier's men from the left centre swiftly joined the action and Guzman's army was dispersed. The attack by the frightened cattle was easily repelled, as the rearguard buccaneers under Bledri Morgan aimed at the faces of the leaders, to turn the stampede back on the Spanish. De Alcaudete was wounded, and only Guzman appeared to remain on the field of battle, attended by a faithful Negro servant and a priest, who entreated him to escape. Guzman reluctantly returned to Panama to marshal the defences, with thirty cannon covering the main streets, but the British and French soon over-ran the disheartened defenders. Casualties had been just five men killed and ten wounded against the Spaniards' four hundred or so. A galleon full of bullion just managed to escape into the wide Pacific, carrying fleeing nobility and clergymen.

One of Morgan's most valuable trophies was a *derrotero*, a Spanish manuscript sea atlas, containing detailed charts and navigational instructions for Pacific coasts and harbours. Its importance is measured by the fact that it is mentioned three times in *The Calendar of State Papers* of the Public Records Office. Although it has disappeared, it may be the ms. HM.918 in the Huntington Library collection.

The retreating Spanish set fire to the main powder magazine in order to ruin the city, but Morgan's followers managed to keep the fires mainly under control for the next three weeks as they plundered the remaining buildings. Much treasure was dredged up from wells, dried out by the raging fires. Esquemeling states that Morgan set fire to Panama, but a letter by Guzman exists stating that it was his order. Morgan wrote to Modyford that the Spanish viceroy '*ordered the city to be fired, and his chief forts to be blown up, the which was in such haste that they blew up 40 of his soldiers in it. We followed into the town, where in the market place they made some resistance and fired some great guns, killed us 4 men and wounded 5.'* The buccaneer William Frogge also stated that the Spaniards, not Morgan set fire to the city. Frogge also complained bitterly about the payout of £10 per man for this expedition, around £2000 in today's money[2]. Such was the destruction that this city was never rebuilt, but another Panama was built, a few miles along the Pacific coast at Perico.

The pirates desperately searched for the famous *Golden Altar of the City of San Jose*, but assumed the escaping *La Santissima Trinidada*[3] had taken it. It was covered with plates of solid beaten gold and worth an enormous sum. According to some sources, priests had covered it

The fighting at Panama

with white paint, which was scraped off several years later. Morgan's men were alleged by Esquemeling to have tortured priests to find its whereabouts, but not much credence can be given to this story. The buccaneers also captured ships and towns in the surrounding Pearl Islands, taking booty and 3,000 prisoners to ransom. Morgan sent out the four fastest ships he could find in Panama harbour, under Robert Searle (released by Modyford to help Morgan), to chase the escaping treasure galleon. However, they only came back with another, smaller barque. At Taboga Island, this merchantman had valuable cargo and a chest with 20,000 pieces of eight. The buccaneers also captured slaves and Panamanian refugees on the island. For a month Morgan's men ravaged the area, torturing prisoners to find the whereabouts of treasure. A particular pleasure was said to be hanging men by their testicles until they told the ruffians what they wanted to hear. Morgan seems to have fallen in love with one of the Spanish ladies travelling on the merchantman. He tried by all methods to seduce her, but, failing, released. Two friars spent her ransom money upon freeing some religious colleagues, so Morgan hung them and sent her on her way on a mule.

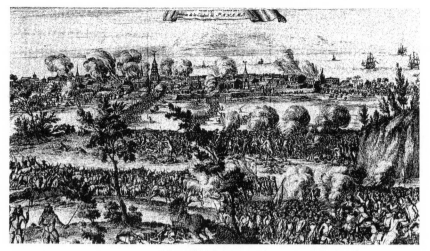

Morgan's sack of Panama

This, again, is Esquemeling's unreliable version of events, and his account of this romance is over three times the length of his actual description of the whole attack on Panama. Morgan himself called it a total fiction. More likely is Surgeon-General Browne's account when he heard of the accusations against Morgan: '*The report from England is very high (over-exaggerated), and a great deal worse than it was: what was done in fight and heat of pursuit of a flying enemy, I presume is pardonable; as to their women I know nor heard of anything offered beyond their wills; something I know was cruelly executed by Captain Collier in killing a friar in the field after quarter given; but (as) for the Admiral he was noble enough to the vanquished enemy.*' Browne noted that the female captives were '*well-treated*', despite the fact that he quarrelled with Morgan after the raid.

So much plunder was taken that some factions of pirates were thinking of escaping with a share of the loot from Panama. Morgan heard of this, and ordered all the vessels dismasted and their sails and rigging burned. The buccaneers were becoming more difficult to control, fewer and fewer riches were coming from tortures, and the flow of ransoms was drying up. On February 14, 1671, the buccaneers loaded up their booty and set off for Chagres. Over 170 mules and horses were loaded down, as were all the captured slaves and Spanish families. At Venta Cruz (Cruces) they stopped to accept some ransoms in the form of meat, maize and rice as well as money. A rumour spread like wildfire among the buccaneers that Morgan was reserving some extra precious trophies, such as a solid gold shrine, for himself. To stamp the incipient mutiny out, Morgan had himself strip-searched and his knapsack inspected, then ordered it to be done to all the rest of his men. Some old-timers and the French resented this bitterly, and disloyal mutterings about Morgan's leadership were still heard. After 12 days, the expedition arrived at San Lorenzo Castle at Chagres, on February 26th. Espinosa's fleet had not been sighted, and Norman's garrison in the fort welcomed him warmly, seeing the vast riches they would share in. Taking advantage of this added strength, Morgan acted quickly and picked out several French ringleaders of the potential mutiny and had them executed.

Morgan now sent the prisoners taken at Old Providence to Puerto Bello. They had been promised their freedom without ransom under the terms Morgan came to with their governor. A message was sent with the ship that San Lorenzo would be destroyed unless the Spanish authorities ransomed it. Don Alfonso de Alcaudete, recovered from his injuries on the plain of Matasnillos, refused to send anything. Morgan demolished the castle, spiking all the guns except the best, which he took for his own ship. Morgan claimed that £30,000 was made in ransoms, but some of the other captains felt that he had made over £70,000 for the share-out at the end of the voyage. W. Llywelyn Williams estimated that the total value of all the plunder, including slaves, was 750,000 pieces of eight, the richest raid in history. Morgan released those Spanish prisoners whose ransoms had not been paid. The normal practice would have been to sell them as slaves. According to Spanish sources the total loss was from 18 million pesos to 6 million crowns.

At Chagres, Admiral Morgan announced that the common pool could only pay out 200 pieces of eight, about £10 at the time, to each soldier and sailor who took part in the expedition, after deductions had been made for the King, the Lord High Admiral, officers, ship-owners, ships' surgeons and the like. All of the French and many English captains sailed off in disgust, to try to get more booty along the coast. Esquemeling was particularly scathing about Morgan's arithmetic. 'Morgan was deaf to all these and many other complaints of this kind, having designed in his mind to cheat them of as much as he could.' Surgeon Browne also complained that Morgan did not give the men their fair share of the booty - he 'cheated the soldjer of a very vast summe.' W. Llywelyn Williams however, thinks the share-out was about right, considering that the payments for injuries were higher than normal, captains took eight shares instead of five, Charles II took 10% and the Duke of York a fifteenth of the total. Henry Morgan's 1% share would have given him 7,500 pieces of eight. The disenchanted Esquemeling left Morgan at this time, to cruise the Honduras before joining the French buccaneers in Tortuga.

On March 12th, Morgan returned to Port Royal as a hero, with just 4 ships of his 35. Another 6 ships sailed into Port Royal shortly after, but his cousin Bledri Morgan sailed from Chagres to Old Providence, where he acted as governor for a time. However, Morgan had captured Chagres after the unofficial news had come to Jamaica that there was peace with Spain. Morgan must have known by December 1st, if only from Spanish captives, but he pleaded utter ignorance. Admiral Morgan submitted his report on April 20th, and appeared before the council of Jamaica on May 31st to relate his voyage to Panama. It is noted that he received the formal congratulations of Modyford, and the approval of the Council of Jamaica for carrying out his commission. Morgan had written in his report to Governor Modyford, *'thus was consumed the famous and ancient city of Panama, the greatest mart for silver and gold in the entire world, for it receives all the goods that come into it from Old Spaine in the King's great fleet and likewise delivers to the fleet all the silver and gold that comes from the mines of Peru and Potosi.'* Modyford's brother wrote *'I think we are well revenged for their burning our houses on ye north and south side of this island.'* The Council met on June 10, 1671 and publicly thanked Morgan for carrying out his commission: *'The Council gave him many thanks for the execution of his last commission and approve very well of his acting therein.'* Henry was rich, happily married (albeit sadly childless) and at the apogee of his fame and influence.

The English Ambassador to Spain wrote *'It is impossible for me to describe the effect of this news upon Madrid.'* The Queen-Regent spent hours on her knees, praying publicly, and all of Spain was in mourning. However, back in London, the Conde de Molina, the Spanish Ambassador to Whitehall, was incensed by Morgan's actions, and wanted him to face trial. Charles II was too weak financially to face another war, and tried to defuse the situation by ordering Sir Thomas Lynch to replace Governor Modyford, and send Modyford home as a prisoner. Charles must have noted Morgan's popularity with the people, and did not want a repetition of his father's fate. Morgan kept his head down, hoping that the King would believe his account of events. Lynch was independently wealthy, and indeed had loaned the king £50,000, probably in exchange for a knighthood. Unlike Modyford, he did not intend operating hand-in-glove with Morgan. The recent Asiento agreement meant that there were fortunes to be made in the slave trade taking Negroes from Africa to the Spanish colonies. He had no need of privateers. Lynch arrived in Jamaica in June, showed his commission to the Council, and arrested Morgan's friend and patron, Governor Modyford. The venal Arlington arrested one of Modyford's two remaining son, Charles and put him in the Tower of London on May 16 as surety that Modyford would comply with Lynch's instructions. The pro-Catholic and pro-Spanish Duke of York, who was later to lose the throne because of the Protestant resistance, told Lynch that he should use his utmost force in *'destroying the privateers.'* The tide had turned for Harry Morgan.

Lynch had to take care in his dealings with Morgan, and seems to have been ambivalent about him. A letter to Lord Arlington written on July 2, 1671, says *'This voyage has mightily lessened and humbled them* (the privateers), *and they would take it for a great compliment to be severe with Morgan, whom they rail on horribly for starving, cheating and deserting them.'* He falsely said that Morgan had lost four-fifths of his men on the expedition, and the survivors *'would take it as a compliment to be severe with Morgan whom they rail (at) horribly for starving, cheating and deserting them.'* However, half of the men from Jamaica had returned in Morgan's first four ships by that time, and more ships were still returning. Also, Lynch's assertion that just the frigate *Assistance* (in which he had arrived, just a week earlier) and a ketch would be enough to *'awe the privateers'* was a pathetic boast.

While Morgan was wracked with fever, on August 15th Lynch invited Modyford and some of the Council of Jamaica on board the *Assistance*. Lynch had been staying, rent-free, at Modyford's house, eating and drinking with him since his arrival. The ship's company were ready, and Lynch arrested the unsuspecting Modyford, *'the soule of Jamaica'*. Governor Modyford was sent to London on August 22nd, in *The Jamaica*

Captains	Prize or Port	Value at the time
Christopher Myngs, with 12 ships and less than 500 men	1663 San Francisco de Campeche, Mexico	150,000 pesos (£37,500)
Edward Morgan with 6 ships and 300 men	1665 Oranjestad, St Eustatius	100,000 pesos (£25,000)
Francis L'Olonnais with 8 ships and 660 men	1667 Several ships, Maracaibo and Gibraltar, Venezuela	260,000 pesos (£65,000)
Henry Morgan with 10 ships and 500 men	1668 Puerto Principe, Cuba; Panama, Portobello	250,000 pesos (£62,500)
Henry Morgan with 8 ships and under 500 men	1669 Maracaibo and Gibraltar, Venezuela	120,000 pesos (£30,000)
Henry Morgan with up to 2000 men	1671 Panama City	120,000 pesos (£30,000)

Merchant, and on his arrival, his hostage son was released. Modyford was kept in some comfort in the Tower of London for two years, then released to return to Jamaica as Chief Justice. Morgan, the hero of the Jamaicans, spent his time drinking and socialising in Port Royal and Santiago de la Vega. The scale and intensity of the raiding along the coast of South America in Morgan's years is incredible.

1672

After Modyford's arrest, Lynch called a meeting of the Council and showed them his orders to arrest Modyford as 'a prisoner of state.' The Council were not swayed, knowing that the sick Morgan was in the deepest of trouble, and insisted on passing a resolution, which confirmed that they had given the commission to Morgan. This was sent to London on *The Jamaica Merchant,* along with Modyford. Lynch had realised the strength of feeling for Morgan on the island and in the Council, and started to plot to hurt Morgan's reputation, which would strengthen his own position.

Morgan was still ill, probably from a disease contracted in the terrible Panama crossing, and Dr Holmes tried to sue him for the loss of his ship *Port Royal* off Chagres. Lynch started hanging privateers, so Esquemeling noted that privateers were not returning to Jamaica, and leaving the island defenceless. Most went to Tortuga, coexisting with its French privateers.

Lynch was now forced into a reversal of policy – he called for a full Council of War, as a Spanish invasion was again believed to be imminent. Morgan was missing, still in his bed. Martial law was declared, but there was no income coming into the island. Trade had dried up because of Lynch's actions, and he was forced to use his own money to repair fortifications. Captain Edward Collier assisted in drawing up plans for the island's defences.

In London, the Spanish ambassador kept pushing for the arrest of Morgan. After Puerto Bello and Maracaibo, Panama was just too much. The King insisted that he had no news of the action, and was waiting for the arrested Modyford to return with the facts of the matter. However, Charles II eventually weakened to Ambassador Molina's insistence, and the veiled threat of a revenge Spanish attack on Jamaica. In January 1672 Lynch received orders to send Morgan home to answer for his offences. Lynch put Morgan on an old royal frigate, the *Welcome,* which he called *'an old vessel, and if taken in any distress of weather would be lost with all her men.'*

He was obviously hoping that the problem would be solved at sea, and on April 4 she set off with the arrested Morgan on board. Although still ill, Morgan had prepared well for the eventuality, having sent to England a long memorandum on the necessity of encouraging privateers where there was no adequate naval protection for the colonies. He also canvassed all his friends for testimonials of recommendation to present to the King. The voyage took three stormy months, and Captain John Keene reported to the cabinet's Lord Clifford that '*the two prisoners are still on board, but very much tired with their long confinement, especially Captain Morgan, who is very sickly.*' After a month at sea, food and water rapidly deteriorate, and there are severe outbreaks of scurvy and enteric illnesses. The admiral was ill when he began the voyage in the tropics, and then confined in a damp cabin for some of its duration. In terrible weather conditions, the ship was saved more than once because Morgan took command of her. He was a vastly more experienced sailor than Keene. Morgan complained that after this voyage, and the oncoming cold and fogs of an English winter, he never regained his health.

Just after Morgan had landed in England, the frightened Lynch suddenly realised the real error of his policy in forcing the privateers, Jamaica's only defence, to leave the island. He had also learned that England was again at war with Spain. He had previously written to the king, '*all may be lost if we have not a frigate or two to defend the island. It is impossible to raise privateers against the Dutch...*'

On his arrival Morgan was immediately released pending trial. Governor Lynch, not Morgan's ally by any means, sent an accompanying letter to London that stated that '*to tell the truth of him, he's an honest, brave fellow, and had both Sir Thomas Modyford's and the Council's commission and instructions, which they thought he obeyed and followed so well they gave him public thanks, which is recorded in the record books. However, it must be confessed that the privateers did divers barbarous acts, which they lay to his Vice-Admiral's account.*' Morgan's vice-admiral was Collier, now Lynch's right-hand man in the defence of Jamaica, which seems ironic. Another letter to Arlington was written by Major-General Bannister, the former Governor of Surinam, and whom Lynch put in charge of defending Jamaica: '*(Morgan) received here a very high and honourable applause for his noble service, both from Sir Thomas Modyford and the Council that commissioned him. I hope without offence I may say he is a very well-deserving person, and one of great courage, who may, with his Majesty's pleasure, perform good public service at home or be very advantageous to this island if war should break forth with the Spaniard.*' Harry Morgan spent his time being feted in London taverns and coffee houses, gambling and going to the races and theatre, and also visited his relatives in Wales. However, he was spending money like water – he had to rent a suitable London house, attend court and live in style.

Modyford was not so fortunate, being confined to a cell in the Tower of London, until released when Morgan arrived. A petition to King Charles had been sent immediately after his arrest, but was rejected by the Privy Council. It had been signed by Admiral Henry Morgan, Colonel Cary and Robert Byndloss, and then 33 of the island's leading merchants, 251 of its leading freeholders, 7 majors and 17 captains.

Charles owed Morgan a great deal for the financial gains he had made, and for the fact that Morgan's victories had been the only success stories in his endeavours against Spain. Morgan was a popular hero in Britain, and between 1672 and 1675 was feted by Court and nobles, was seen smoking in fashionable coffeehouses, and also spent plenty of time in the dockside taverns and brothels where he probably felt more at home. John Evelyn, a Member of the new Commission for Trade and Plantations, noted in his Diary on August 19, 1671 about Panama, that '*The letters of Sir Tho. Modyford were read, giving relation of the exploit at Panama, which was very brave; they took, burnt and pillaged ye town of vast treasures, but the best of the booty had been shipped off and lay at anchor in the South sea, so that after our men had ranged the country 60 miles about, they went back to Nombre de Dios, and embarked for Jamaica. Such an action has not been done since the famous Drake.*' Morgan and Modyford were feted everywhere, and Morgan told Evelyn at a dinner that with a thousand men he could capture the whole of the Spanish Indies for the King. The Third Dutch War had broken out, however, and every ship was needed to guard Britain.

Morgan met Christopher, Duke of Albemarle, the son of General Monck, and a relative of Modyford. Albemarle had helped with the release of Modyford from gaol, and promised he would also help Morgan. The Duke was close to Charles II because his father had engineered the return of the King to replace Richard Cromwell and the Reformation Government. Morgan was 37 and Albemarle 19, and they became life-long friends. The younger man seemed to recognise that Morgan had a great deal to teach him. Although the third richest man in England, after the King and the Duke of York, Albemarle was a kindred spirit to Morgan. He was married to Lady Ogle, but before Morgan arrived had been involved in a serious scandal. Whetstone Park was a low-class area of *bordels* (brothels) and *grog-shops* (taverns). Albemarle had gone to a brothel there on a Saturday night with some lesser lords, and the Duke of Somerset and the Duke of Monmouth (the same Monmouth who later led the bloody Monmouth Rebellion). A beadle (assistant constable) tried to enter the bordel to suppress the drunken noise and shenanigans, and was killed by a sword, allegedly by Albemarle. There was an outcry by the people of London, but Charles pardoned all the offenders, who continued to use Whetstone Park.

In 1672, Major-General Banister, Commander-in-Chief of the troops in Jamaica, wrote to Lord Arlington in Morgan's defence that Morgan '*is a well deserving person, and one of great courage and conduct, who may, with His Majesty's pleasure, perform good public service at home, or be very advantageous to this island if war should break out against the Spaniards.*' Arlington was one of King Charles' inner cabinet. All of Charles' closest advisors except Arlington were now in the pro-Morgan faction at court. In the light of Lynch's despatches from Jamaica, Morgan was now asked by a reluctant Arlington what was needed to save the colony – the island only had the *Assistance* frigate as its defence. Morgan asked for 20 cannon for the new batteries at Port Royal, and a 5th-rate frigate to take him home.

1673 THE TRIAL

Morgan was tiring of London. It was soaking up his fortune[4], and there seemed to be no sight of a trial. He complained directly to the king that he wanted a hearing. There was no formal trial. Morgan and others gave evidence informally to the Lords of Trade and Plantations (which later became the Colonial Office), and the evidence was submitted to King Charles II. Modyford could prove that he had sent a messenger to the Isle des Vaches to tell Morgan that there was a truce with Spain. Morgan could prove that the messages were returned to Jamaica with their seals unbroken. The messenger had '*disappeared*', either by accident or design. No members of the expedition were called to account, to say where Morgan was when the messages were allegedly delivered. Morgan was then called before Charles to give a personal account, and answer a few questions. Deliberately or not, there was no real evidence against Morgan or Modyford.

In the dossier of evidence, there were some complaints, mainly about the sharing of booty, but his relative at the great Tredegar House in Monmouthshire, William Morgan, wrote strongly on his behalf about his '*relation and former near neighbour.*' '*He has had a very good character of him, and in the management of the late business of Panama he behaved with as much prudence, fidelity and resolution as could reasonably be expected, and at his return his services were approved by the then Governor and Council, and thanks ordered him, and all good men would be troubled if a person of his loyalty and consideration as to His Majesty's affairs in those parts should fall for want of friends to assist him.'* It was almost as if Morgan himself had written the letter. Intriguingly at this time, Henry's father Robert was known to be in London, from 1671-1676, but as yet there is no evidence of their meetings.

Morgan's lobbying of past favours also had resulted in this evidence for the defence, from Major-General Banister, Commander of the Forces in Jamaica, and a member of the Council. Morgan had received *'a very high and honourable applause for his noble service therein, both from Sir Thomas Modyford and the Council that commissioned him.'* Albemarle[5], one of the most powerful political figures in England, had also lobbied tirelessly for his friend Morgan's acquittal. The only real danger to Morgan had come from the Spanish Ambassador. Even if Morgan had not known about the Treaty of Madrid, his commission did not give him the authority to fight on land and sack Panama City. Morgan's defence was that a phrase in his commission enabled him to *'do all manner of exploits'* in order to pay his men with captured goods and merchandise.

One of the English ministerial secretaries raised the point that by marching and giving battle in military formation, Morgan had *'arrogated the privileges of His Majesty's Army'* and thus made an official act of war. Morgan casually responded that he had to complete the work of Porto Bello, and prevent further attacks upon English shipping and upon Jamaica, indeed it had been *'a war to end war.'* The *'pestiferous nest'* of Panama had to be wiped out to stop Spanish aggression. He was also asked why he did not believe the Spanish when they told him that there was peace between the countries. Morgan replied that he had forgotten if anyone had told him that. He went on to say that he would have disbelieved it anyway, as all his experience showed him that the Spanish were liars. It was at this point that Charles was supposed to have said *'Oddsfish!'* and exploded with laughter, concluding the hearing.

As well as Albemarle, the Duke of Monmouth was a drinking companion of Morgan's. Monmouth was Charles' 'illegitimate' son by Lucy Walters, but was probably legitimate, and the heir to the throne (see the author's *'100 Great Welsh Women*). Morgan was wildly popular with the people of Britain, especially in London. He moved easily in Court circles. Charles had gained enormous riches from Morgan's expeditions. His brother James, Duke of York, as Admiral of the Fleet, had also made a fortune (although he was himself a Catholic).[6] Charles quickly consulted with James and his inner advisors, the infamous *Cabal* of the lords Clifford, Arlington, Buckingham, Ashley and Lauderdale. They risked losing Jamaica to the Spanish or Dutch. They had replaced the efficient Modyford with the panicking Lynch. Morgan was needed back in Jamaica to restore confidence and lead its sea defences. The verdict was obviously '*not proven*'. Morgan's luck had held again, and the public reception was ecstatic. A few days later, King Charles summoned Henry to Court and knighted him. On November 20th, 1673, Charles II received Henry Morgan at Court in Whitehall, and gave him a jewelled snuffbox with the face of Charles set in diamonds. (This was last known in the possession of a descendant of Morgan's brother-in-law, Robert Byndloss, in 1832). Morgan spent more and more time at court, looking for a suitable position back home in Jamaica, where his wife had remained. The island had grown to a population of over 17,000, but was still not safe from the Spanish.

Footnotes:

1. Of course, the *Port Royal* should not have been at this engagement.

2. The historian Edward Long in the 18th century estimated that Morgan's loot between 1669 and 1671 was as follows: Puerto del Principe 50,000 pieces of eight; Porto Bello 250,000 pieces; Maracaibo 250,000 pieces; and Panama 400,000 pieces - almost a million pieces of eight in three years. He went on '*Beside an immense quantity of silks, linen, gold and silver, lace, plate, jewels and other valuable commodities, which probably amounted to near as much more. By this means money grew to be in vast plenty, and returns easy to England, into which many hundred thousand of those pieces of eight were imported.*'

3. Morgan had issued strict orders for the capture of this treasure ship, but they were disobeyed and it managed to escape before he could organise a chasing fleet of captured ships from panama and Perico. It was loaded with gold and silver ingots from Peru for the journey across the Pacific to Spain, and nuns and priests had filled it with the wealth of their churches as Morgan advanced across the Isthmus. If it had been captured, the financial benefits of the raid might have been five-fold, Esquemeling would not have written his libel, and Morgan would be world-famous as a great general and admiral. Also it must be noted that Morgan '*checked his men forcibly when they would have taken ship from Panama to carry buccaneering all the way down the (Pacific) coast – since, unlike them, he had to consider the political repercussions of such an extended seaborne raid.*' (Jack Beeching, introduction to the Alexis Brown translation to Exquemelin's '*The Buccaneers of America.*'

4. Thomas Dalby wrote in 1690, in his account of the history of the West Indies (just 25 years after Morgan's release from charges), '*Without being charged of any crime, or even brought to a hearing, he was kept here at his own expense above three years, not only to the wasting of some thousands he was then worth, but to the hindrance of his planting, and improvement of his fortune by his industry... so that under those difficulties and the perpetual malice of a prevailing court faction, he wasted the remaining part of his life, oppressed not only by those but (also) a lingering consumption, the coldness of this climate and his vexations had brought him into, when he was forced to stay here.*' At this time, it was indeed cold in an English winter – the Thames used to regularly freeze over, allowing people to skate.

5. Albemarle was formerly General Monck, the close friend of Major-General Thomas Morgan, the uncle of Henry Morgan. He died in August 1673, and his young son became a close friend of Morgan.

6. With King Charles' Declaration of Indulgence, the country reacted. It was seen as a stepping-stone in a return to Catholicism. It was withdrawn and replaced by the Test Act where no Catholic could hold office, and James, Duke of York, lost his position as Lord High Admiral. Two members of the ruling cabal, Clifford and Ashley, also lost powers. A Board of the Admiralty of 15 members replaced James, and its first secretary was Samuel Pepys.

CHAPTER VIII

1674

On January 24th, Charles appointed Charles Howard, Earl of Carlisle as Governor of Jamaica, to replace Lynch, the man who had arrested Morgan. On the same day, Sir Henry Morgan was made Lieutenant-Governor of Jamaica. The letter confirming the appointment stated that Charles *'reposed particular confidence in his loyalty, prudence and courage, and long experience of the Colony.'* These words were actually written by the philosopher John Locke, who was then Secretary to the Council of Trade and Plantations. (Locke's *'Treatise on Civil Government'* influenced the American and French revolutionaries). In June, Sir Henry Morgan was also made Lieutenant-General of Jamaica's armed forces, and local command over the king's men-of-war as and when they arrived at Port Royal. Unfortunately Carlisle, a friend of Morgan's, wished to postpone his Governorship of the West Indies, and Lord John Vaughan was commissioned instead. Sir Henry's commission was then changed to make Vaughan his superior. Samuel Pepys described the Welshman Vaughan as *'one of the lewdest fellows of the age'*, and his relations with Morgan were not going to be easy. The Duke of Clarendon called Vaughan *'a person of as ill fame as ill face'*, and Dryden wrote a play dedicated to Vaughan, set in a brothel. Vaughan was a member of the notorious Kit-Kat Club in London. In this year, 1200 settlers arrived from Surinam, and began sugar planting, a key to Jamaica's future wealth.

John Evelyn noted in his diary that Sir Thomas Modyford and Colonel Morgan were being entertained at Lord Berkeley's on September 21st, 1674. On October 20th, Evelyn met Morgan and Modyford and recorded: *'London: Council, dined with * at my Lord Berkely's where I had discourse with Sir Thomas Modyford, late Governor of Jamaica, and with Colonel Morgan who undertook that gallant exploit from Nombre de Dios to Panama on the Continent of America: he told me 10000 men would easily conquer all the Spanish Indies, they were so secure: great was the booty they took, and much, nay infinitely greater had it been, had they not been betrayed and so discovered before their approach, as they had time to carry on board the vast Treasure, which they put off to sea, in sight of our Men, that they had no boats to follow, etc: They set fire to Panama, and ravaged the country 60 miles about.'*

The two great friends, Morgan and Modyford, were on their way 'home'. Sir Thomas Modyford had been appointed Chief-Justice of Jamaica. They obviously thought that they could easily 'sort out' Vaughan and once again control the island. The deposed Governor, Sir Thomas Lynch, was mortified that the two men he had arrested were coming back, Morgan laden with honours. In November 1674 he wrote to the Lords of Trade and Plantations about the increasing Spanish threat, no doubt hoping to rescind Charles' decisions 'One of the reasons of their coming is the noise of Admiral Morgan's favour at Court and return to the Indies, which much alarmed the Spaniards, and caused the King to be at vast charge in fortifying in the South Sea.' The Spanish had allowed their governors in the West Indies to begin issuing commissions, mainly because their warships there had either been wrecked, or destroyed by Morgan, and they themselves were defenceless against privateers.

1675
THE WRECK OF THE JAMAICA MERCHANT

By a wonderful irony, the ship that carried Morgan and Modyford to Jamaica in pomp was the *Jamaica Merchant*, which had taken Modyford to London as a prisoner back in 1671. Modyford was part-owner of the vessel. On January 8, the frigate *Foresight* containing Vaughan and *The Jamaica Merchant* weighed anchor. The *Jamaica Merchant* was loaded with the 20 cannon, powder and shot that Morgan had requested. Vaughan gave explicit instructions that they should keep close touch. Morgan and Vaughan seem to have hated each other from the start. Vaughan knew he had a larger-than-life character to keep in order. Morgan saw Vaughan as an inconvenience to his plans, a highly literate court dandy. The ships were separated on the first day out from England, for which Vaughan seems to have blamed Morgan. Morgan claimed that the anchor was stuck fast, and that Vaughan was out of range before they could set off. Although ostensibly on the same course, the ships never sighted each other again. The *Jamaica Merchant* made an incredibly fast crossing, not to Jamaica but to Morgan's old haunt of the Isle des Vaches. (How on earth a bulky merchantman loaded with cannon made better sail than a naval frigate is a matter for conjecture. The *Foresight* was brand-new, built for speed, with a clean bottom). Morgan took over command of the ship, and completed the crossing in a record 6 weeks, half the time it had taken to reach London.

Morgan obviously wanted to meet someone at his favourite rendezvous, but also get to Jamaica before Lynch. However, on February 25th, his ship was wrecked in a huge storm at the Isle des

Facsimile of a letter written by Sir Henry Morgan 'The Buccaneer' to Captain Edmunds. Dated at Port Royal, Jamaica, 25th August 1675.

Vaches. Captain Knapman claimed that he had not meant to be there at all. Whether the loss was contrived, we do not know. Perhaps Morgan (and Modyford) were picking up some hidden loot that had been stashed away in case things went awry in London.[1] An alternative theory is that Modyford wanted the ship wrecked to claim insurance upon it.

Morgan later wrote to England that *'we had all perished, had I not known where I was'*. After a few days, Captain Thomas Rogers on the *Gift* landed. He had a French commission to attack the Spanish as those countries were now at war, and he had served under Morgan at Panama. (Rogers was involved in a skirmish with Spanish ambushers on the 6th day of the march across the isthmus). He picked the newly ennobled Morgan, Modyford and the crew up, and he was in Port Royal on March 5th, still an astonishing nine days before the arrival of Vaughan's faster frigate, which had come the direct and quicker route. Morgan was a clever man, who would have been called a *'dashing rogue'* in romantic potboilers. Welcomed in the taverns of Port Royal, Morgan rode almost immediately the twelve miles to the capital of St Jago, where with great relish he demanded a meeting of the Council, which was held on March 7th. Sir Henry Morgan must have smiled when he gave his commission and formally deposed the bitter Governor Thomas Lynch. He asked the Council if he could assume the Governorship and take command of the island, and took the chair for the rest of the meeting. On March 11th, at another Council meeting in Port Royal, Morgan received the Great Seal of the Island, formally granting him the Governorship and authority to act. He had inspected the island's defences and found them to be woeful, fortifications were crumbling and stocks of powder and shot would not last over three hours.

However, a vengeful Lord Vaughan finally arrived in Jamaica on March 14th, 9 days after Morgan, and the first of Morgan's terms of Governorship ended the next day. His Atlantic crossing had taken nine weeks, compared to Morgan's six. Vaughan hurriedly summoned a Council in Port Royal, took the Governor's oath, and Henry Morgan was sworn in as his Lieutenant. For the next three years the dour intellectual Vaughan argued constantly with the flamboyant hero Morgan. Morgan had almost immediately accused Lynch of impropriety with a Negro prize-ship, writing to England and calling him *'the greatest cheat of the age'*. Vaughan allied with Lynch against Morgan, and said *'In the Downs I gave him orders, in writing, to keep me company, and in no case to be separated from me but by distress of weather; however he, God knows by what fate, coveting to be here before me, wilfully lost me.'*

Lord Vaughan (National Portrait Gallery)

Rubbing salt into the festering wound of Morgan's popularity, the local parliament had granted him £600 '*for his good services to the country during his Lieutenant-Governorship, but none to his successors*'. The joyous Morgan then appeared on the Parliament floor to thank the representatives, which infuriated his fellow-Welshman Vaughan enough to write home '*His particular ill conduct and wilful breach of his positive and written orders since the meeting at the Assembly, with other follies, have so tired me that I am perfectly weary of him, and I frankly tell you that I think it is for His Majesty's service he should be removed, and the charge (expense) of so useless an officer saved.*'

Morgan now stayed away from the jibes of Vaughan and the capital of St Jago de la Vega as much as possible, sticking to his old friends in Port Royal. Vaughan saw him as being head of a '*de facto*' second capital of the island. On September 20, 1675, Vaughan again wrote to Secretary of State Williamson telling tales: '*I am every day more convinced of his imprudence and unfitness to have anything to do with the Civil Government, and of what hazards the Island may run with so dangerous a succession. Sir Henry has made himself and his authority so cheap at the Port, drinking and gaming at the taverns, that I intend to remove thither speedily myself for the reputation of the Island and the security of the place.*' Lord Vaughan was never made welcome at Port Royal, and never stayed for long, however. The Secretary of State showed little sympathy, and instead wrote to ask Morgan, not Vaughan, for a report on conditions upon the colony. Morgan answered that Vaughan would not let him contribute in Jamaica's government, so he could only send an incomplete account, but that he was as ready as any man to obey his King's commands.

1676

With Morgan's two plantations at Lawrencefield and Morgan's Valley prospering, he bought another 4000 acres at St Elizabeth for planting sugar. In early spring, Sir Henry had halted the execution of a privateer called Deane, and Vaughan believed that he was also sending warnings to buccaneers rather than arresting them. By May he thought he had proof of Morgan's traitorous intentions, and wrote again to Secretary of State Williamson: '*What I most resent is, and which I consider as parts of my duty to lay before your Honour, that I find Sir Henry, contrary to his duty and trust, endeavours to set up privateering, and has obstructed all my designs for the reducing of those that do use that curse of life.*'

Trying desperately to overthrow his second-in-command, the embittered Vaughan also wrote to the Lord Privy Seal, Lord Anglesea: '*I detected him (Morgan) of a most gross unfaithfulness in his trust, and a wilful breach and disobedience of my orders, only because they have obstructed his design of privateering....Since the trial of Deane he has been so impudent and unfaithful at the taverns and in his own house..... and has, with his brother (in-law) Byndloss, encouraged the King's subjects to take French commissions, fitted them out to sea, and been concerned with them in their ships and prizes. I know his imprudence and weakness lead him a long way, but believe his necessities do more, which would prove of sad consequence to the Island if there should be any devolution of Government.... His brother Byndloss agitates him in all he does, and I have therefore given him (Byndloss) no authority of any civil or military commission. He is a turbulent fellow, some years since he was surgeon of a ship, but never can be easy in any Government. It would be a good thing if the Governor had a private instruction to put him out of the Council.*'

Lieutenant-Colonel Robert Byndloss was now Morgan's only open supporter on the eight-man Council of Jamaica, and this was Vaughan's last throw of the dice to get rid of this pair of scoundrels, who seemed to be openly flouting his authority. It was obvious at this time that Morgan was '*sailing close to the wind*' in his dealings with his former buccaneer associates. It was another thing for Vaughan to prove it, but he hurriedly called the Council together on July 24, 1676. Morgan was not invited and knew nothing of it. Byndloss was told to be present, because the Council wanted to ask him about his taking the French government's commission off Tortugan privateers. At the meeting, Vaughan produced letters showing that Morgan had issued privateering commissions. He was furious with Morgan, as the Admiralty Court consisted of Morgan, Byndloss and Colonel Beeston. Vaughan had ordered a slave ship to be condemned as a prize, and the Court had over-ruled him, and dismissed the case.

MORGAN'S SECOND TRIAL

Whatever one feels about Admiral Sir Henry Morgan as a character, one cannot but admire his almost mischievous self-confidence. His humour tempered his natural arrogance, and this trial also shows his intelligence

Sir Henry Morgan

and native Welsh cunning. At the trial called by Lynch, Morgan quietly sat through the list of charges, and was interrogated for a couple of hours by his peers on the Council. Vaughan became quite vehement as he tried to rattle Sir Henry into making a mistake in his eloquent, and sometimes sophisticated answers. After all, Henry had been questioned by the King and the greatest in the land and found innocent of all charges. This jumped-up *land-lubber* was not going to get under his skin, instead he would slowly reel Vaughan in and watch him squirm. On the charge that Morgan had corresponded with '*monsieurs Puncay and Cussy*', intending to collaborate with them to attack Spain, Vaughan had written proof. Also Morgan was known to have met on several occasions, in the drinking dens of Port Royal, with a French privateer named Prinier.

Things looked black for the old freebooter, but his answer was easy and assured. The Sieur de Pouancey (Puncay) had succeeded his uncle d'Ogeron as Governor of Tortuga and Western Hispaniola. The Comte de Cussy was de Pouancey's lieutenant, eventually to succeed him as Governor. They were the employees of Louis XIV, with whom Charles II had excellent relations. As a fellow senior official in the West Indies, what was wrong with diplomatic relations? If relations with the French were forbidden, where was the written order? Were there any minutes or documents to prove this? Did anyone on the Council know of such an edict? (Morgan, when debarred from giving commissions to privateers, had sent them on to his friend d'Ogeron, and received a monetary commission from him, via Byndloss).

On the next charge of talking to the French pirate Prinier, Morgan explained that he was just carrying out political subterfuge. He wished to make sure through this man and his colleagues that the French were not issuing commissions to buccaneers. How else could he find out? By this time the majority of the Council were sensing a sea-change in the relative positions of authority of Lord Vaughan and Admiral Morgan. Morgan went on to offer his secretary's deposition that Morgan was totally innocent of dealing with privateers for his own ends. Morgan stated that Vaughan had never confided in him, and was out to ruin him '*for what reasons I know not.*' He finished his speech as follows: '*If I err in one tittle (small piece), then let me ever be condemned for the greatest villain in the world … I suckled the milk of loyalty, and if I would have sold one little part of it I might have been richer than my enemies will ever be.*'

Morgan sat down, satisfied and asked for some tobacco and rum while he watched the proceedings against Byndloss. While less loquacious, Byndloss gave the same, probably rehearsed, story. (Byndloss's descendants were left a fortune by Morgan in his will, on condition they took Morgan's surname in perpetuity, probably to make up for Morgan and his beloved Mary Elizabeth being unable to have children). The transcript of this executive enquiry was then sent to London, where Morgan's lobby was far closer to the locus of power than Vaughan's. The Council had seen that there was effectively no case to answer, and while the status quo reigned until Whitehall came to a decision, they knew that Vaughan had lost the running battle. The Privy Council passed on all the documentation from Vaughan, the Council, Morgan and Byndloss to the Lords of Trade. Around this time also, the Lords of Trade and Plantations decided that the alleged pirate Deane was tried improperly, and ordered his release.

1677

Vaughan and Morgan both added to their plantations. Vaughan must have been assured of his victory over Morgan, as he now held the greatest estate in Jamaica. However, with just the *Foresight* to protect the colony, he was receiving information of Spanish attacks commissioned by the Governor of Havana. His reports back to London showed that Lynch's policy of appeasement had not worked, and that the people of Jamaica had no faith in the Crown's ability to protect them. Of course, this was good news for Morgan and the privateers. When new came to London that the *Diligence* had been taken, in time of peace, the Spanish ambassador was asked to explain the action at Whitehall. He replied that a Captain John Barnett had taken a Spanish ship off Hispaniola, carrying 46,000 pieces of eight. Thomas Lynch, now in London, informed the Privy Council that this was a French ship with a French crew, flying the French flag and with a French commission, which sold the prize and divided the spoils in a French port, and was thus nothing to do with England or Jamaica. Further despatches from Lynch about more English ships being taken again hardened the attitude at court.

The Earl of Carlisle was also receiving correspondence from islanders, stating that Morgan and Byndloss were indispensable to the protection of the island. (Carlisle should have replaced Lynch as Governor, and was still pondering whether to take the post). Morgan wrote to London in support of Byndloss, and asked if there was to be another trial that he (Morgan) could be tried by his peers at the Court of King's Bench in Jamaica, where all the witnesses were, rather than ruin his health once again on the Atlantic crossing.

In summer 1677, the official verdict on Morgan's trial came back to Jamaica. It was that The Lords of Trade and the Plantations had come to no resolution of the matter and would examine the case further. The Lords, along with Charles' Court, looked upon Morgan, now known as 'The Sword of England', as the deputy for his friend the Earl of Carlisle. Vaughan was seen as a stopgap Governor, holding the seat for Carlisle, and in the winter he was recalled as Carlisle decided to take up the office. Sir Harry had won the political and diplomatic battle at last. Morgan had been vindicated over Vaughan, and when this verdict reached Jamaica in Autumn, most of the Council now openly sided with Morgan. Indeed, Vaughan was over-ruled on procedural matters by the island's Assembly, which refused to pass a bill, and so he had no funding to run his island's administration. In retaliation, he wrote to London asking for permission to suspend Council of Jamaica members, calling some of them 'old Standers and officers of Cromwell's army' thus trying to appeal to the king.

Next, Captain Browne sailed from Port Royal with a French commission against the Dutch. Browne captured the Dutch ship Golden Sun, and sold 150 of its slave cargo to planters in Jamaica. Vaughan told the Admiralty Court to confiscate the slaves and charge Captain Browne with breaking the Royal Africa Company's monopoly of the slave trade with the island. Most of the Council and Assembly were against him. The Assembly had passed a law allowing Browne to sail into Port Royal and not be prosecuted, but Vaughan was determined to hang him as an example. The Assembly passed a resolution delaying the execution, but within half-an-hour the vindictive Vaughan had hanged him, enraging most people of importance in Jamaica.

1678 MORGAN'S SECOND TERM

On January 13, Carlisle received his commission, and in March Vaughan left Jamaica forever. Among his last acts were halving Harry Morgan's salary to £300 and dismissing the Assembly. On April 3, Morgan was sworn in as Acting Governor in Port Royal. He was alerted to a possible French attack – they had recaptured Cayenne from the Dutch. He immediately called a Council meeting and was appointed commander-in-chief. His council of war declared martial law, took military inventories and planned for two new forts to protect Port Royal. Sir Harry's new forts were built by requisitioning a tenth of all Negro slaves on the island, and modelled on the great fortifications he had seen in his buccaneering days. The existing Fort Charles was strengthened, supported by the Morgan Battery and Fort James. The two new forts were named Fort Rupert and Fort Carlisle. A ship had sailed in to Port Royal from London, stating that war was imminent, and that Carlisle was soon on his way there as Governor. After a third Council of War, there came the welcome news that the great French fleet had been wrecked at Bird Island – of 8 men-of-war, 8 frigates, and over a dozen privateers, only a couple of ships survived. (Three of France's new ships of the line had 168 cannon between them.) Once again Morgan's luck had held out. Morgan returned to his main estate at Lawrencefield, once again the hero of Jamaica.

One of the new Privy Councillors was Sir Thomas Modyford, Morgan's old comrade. Chief Justice Modyford had used his 'cuts' from privateering voyages that he had commissioned, probably replacing Vaughan as the richest plantation owner in Jamaica. For three months Sir Henry ruled the island, until the Earl of Carlisle arrived. Carlisle had previously received a confidential report underlining Morgan's popularity on the island, with the added benefit that Morgan always spoke well of Carlisle. Carlisle's problem was that he was not keen upon taking the position. Whitehall had decided to strip powers from the island's Assembly and replace them with laws made in London, after seeing the feud between Vaughan and Lynch on one side and the Council and Assembly on the other. Whitehall had given Carlisle the odious job of stripping independence from the island.

From 1678-80, Morgan stood on the sidelines, not wishing to become embroiled in a bitter political battle between Carlisle and the Council. He was a friend of Carlisle's but a friend of Jamaica far more. Carlisle had been instructed by Charles II to change the pattern of law making on the island, to standardise it with English law. The Assembly of the island could no longer make laws, but merely ratify Whitehall legislation, and could not reject any laws. The Council resented this, sending two Councillors to Whitehall to argue their case, and the Council was suspended. Morgan kept his counsel, remaining neutral in the dispute and waiting to see which way the wind was blowing. In October, Carlisle dissolved the Assembly. Morgan now managed to get Carlisle to send the naval frigate *Jersey*, upon which he had sailed from London, to salvage all 22 guns, and 212 cannon balls from the *Jamaica Merchant* off Ile des Vaches, and carried on with organising the island's defences.

1679

Upon July 7th, two French men-of-war sailed into Port Royal, and were hit at least twice by cannon balls. In response, they fired 7 shot into the town, and sailed off. Carlisle rode to join Morgan and they spent that night waiting for another French invasion fleet. At dawn the French could be seen, and one frigate detached itself from the squadron of eight ships and approached Port Royal. A boat containing the Comte d'Evreaux and some other officers rowed into the port, and the frigate hove off to rejoin the fleet. The Comte stated that the Count d'Estrees' fleet needed water and provisions to battle the Spanish, but Morgan and Carlisle were cautious. They did not want the French to see Port Royal's new defences, and after a day the French rejoined the fleet, which sailed off.

A letter written from Barbados to Modyford stated that it was the intention of the French to take Jamaica, which sparked real anger amongst the plantation owners. In exile, Charles had promised its return to Spain, so feelings were running high, and in desperation, Carlisle recalled the Assembly. The Council and Assembly set up a committee to report on what extra defences were needed, under the chairmanship of Henry Morgan. Morgan immediately wrote the document, wanting four fireships made ready, extra trenches dug to shelter musketeers, two ships permanently ready for action to fire across low land and cover the harbour entrance, new gun platforms and a new fort. The new fort was called Fort Morgan, and the trenches around it Morgan's Lines. The French fleet was sighted again, and the Spanish started taking British merchant shipping.

On Carlisle's arrival, Morgan had resumed his role of Lieutenant Governor, and senior member of the Council. He built up his plantation interests, which were Penkarne in St George, Arthur's Land in St Mary, Danke's Land and Morgan's Valley. He became Judge-Admiral and first 'Custos Rotulorum' (the equivalent of a county's Lord Lieutenant, the 'first citizen') of Port Royal. Unfortunately his friend Modyford, around seventy years old, died in 1679, about which time Morgan was drinking copious amounts even by his notable standards. The tombstone reads: 'Mistake not reader, for here lyes not only the Deceased Body of the Honourable Thomas Modyford but even the soule and life of all Jamaica who first made it what it is now. Here lyes the best and longest Governor, the most considerable planter, the ablest and most upright judge this Island ever enjoyed. He died the Second of September 1679.' Modyford was buried in St Catherine's Church, Spanish Town, and just six weeks later his son and heir Thomas died, the title passing to the younger son Charles. Also in

October, the Assembly rejected London's new laws. Robert Byndloss, Morgan's brother-in-law, became Chief Justice.

Matters were deteriorating across the Caribbean. Many of the Campeche log-cutters, angry at the lack of protection from Jamaica, had turned to piracy. In the autumn of 1679, Captain Peter Harris captured a 28-gun Dutch ship, and Carlisle ordered the frigate *Success* to capture it. However, in the chase the *Success* hit a reef, as Harris navigated expertly through the South Cays off the south of Cuba. Jamaica's only man-of-war was wrecked, so Carlisle had its captain flogged and jailed. Carlisle asked the Privy Council to return to London to discuss the position of Jamaica, appointing Morgan to head a commission upon the protection of trading ships against piracy. Morgan wrote the report, requesting two 6th-rate frigates that could operate in the shallow waters of the Caribbean. The Earl took Sir Harry's report with him to the Privy Council.

1680 THIRD GOVERNORSHIP

In May 1680, the Earl of Carlisle left Jamaica, and Morgan succeeded him. Carlisle had appreciated Morgan's value so much that he thereafter gave him £600 annually from his private purse, saying that '*with his generous humour, I know that (otherwise) he will become a beggar.*' As Carlisle had dissolved the Assembly, Morgan was now in complete control of Jamaica. (Unfortunately for him, Vaughan and Lynch were now in London, actively plotting his downfall). New elections could not be called until the two suspended Council members returned from London. Morgan packed the Council with his own supporters, and ruled for a year as a semi-dictator. His brother in laws Byndloss and Archbold were on the Council, and Robert Byndloss was Chief Justice. His third brother-in-law Charles Byndloss was Commandant of Port Royal. His friend Roger Elletson was Attorney-General and on the Privy Council. Vice-Admiral Sir Henry Morgan was now acting Governor, Lieutenant-General, Justice of the Peace, Chief Judge of the Admiralty Court and still Colonel-Commander of the Port Royal Regiment. Elletson later called this year of Morgan's rule, Jamaica's '*golden age.*'

For some reason, possibly previously agreed with Carlisle, Harry clamped down severely on all privateering. Morgan had huge debts, and saw his way to financial salvation by trading with Spain, rather than warring with it. Some of his debts were incurred by his sponsoring a great new church, St Peters, near the new Fort Morgan in *Morgan's Lines* at Port Royal.

Port Royal was closed to '*illegal*' vessels, and all privateers were offered to apply for pardons. Those who did not apply would be arrested, tried at the Admiralty Court, and hung. In July 1680, Morgan wrote to London asking for some small, quick frigates to stamp out the French buccaneers of Hispaniola, who were attracting Englishmen to become 'brethren of the coast'. Morgan heard of a strange ship in port. He invited the crew to dine with him, and over the free-flowing wine, out-vied them in buccaneering tales. They divulged the whereabouts of Spanish ships that were worth taking. Next morning, on leaving Morgan's hospitality, they were arrested by soldiers. After a short court hearing, seventeen pirates were 'swung off' at the end of the day. In the meantime, Samuel Long and Colonel William Beeston had argued successfully in Whitehall for a return to the Jamaican Constitution. Jamaicans could now self-rule on the same basis as Barbadians.

However, Carlisle and Henry were under attack in London from Vaughan and Lynch. Charles Morgan and Carlisle sent their warnings to Sir Harry, along with the new Secretary of State, fellow-Welshman Sir Leoline Jenkins from Cowbridge in Glamorgan. Henry wrote to London with every ship that went there, making his case that he was suppressing privateers, and receiving thanks from the various Spanish governors, while again buying up more lands. Near Port Maria, he accumulated 1200 acres, which he called Llanrumney, after his birthplace.

1681

In February 1681, Morgan could issue a writ to hold Assembly elections, and worked feverishly to get the new assembly to agree to seven years' of 'contributions' to the London government of Charles II. In the Caribbean, the Dutch Captain Jacob Evertsen was causing havoc with his crew of 64 British and 6 Spanish pirates, and the frigate Norwich could not find him. In January Morgan heard that Evertsen was anchored with a captured brigantine in a Bull Bay near Port Royal, and sent a small merchant sloop with two dozen men of his Port Royal Regiment, and a few small coasters with more soldiers on board. Evertsen allowed the seemingly innocent fleet to come near, smelling easy prey, but was quickly overwhelmed. 26 pirates were captured, but Evertsen managed to swim ashore with most of his crew.

The escapees were rounded up, and the Spaniards were diplomatically despatched to Cartagena for its Governor to deal with them. In March, Morgan as head of the Admiralty Court, announced the death sentence for Evertsen and 60 British pirates, but did not execute them. Morgan reasoned to the Lords of Trade that this action would have prevented many privateers from coming into Port Royal and accepting pardons. However, despite Morgan's excellent record as Governor of Jamaica, the plotting against him in London, inspired by the treacherous Francis Mingham (whose ship Morgan had once confiscated) and fomented by Lynch and Vaughan, meant that the Lords of Trade appointed Lynch Governor of Jamaica in July 1681. Lynch had passed a £50,000 bribe to King Charles II, and the pathetic Stuart monarch used the money to ease the financial situation caused by his whoring lifestyle. He showed no feeling for his heroic contemporary, *'the Sword of England'*, who had been keeping his Caribbean colonies in English hands and contributing to his coffers for decades. In August, Morgan wrote to Sir Leoline Jenkins protesting strongly against the consideration that the Port Royal Regiment be disbanded. Sir Harry was astonished to discover at the end of the year that his old enemy Sir Thomas Lynch had again been given the Governorship, with Morgan becoming once again Lieutenant-Governor.

1682

The new Governor arrived in the frigate *Sweepstake* in May, 1682. Lynch had left his wife and son in Madeira, as they were ill, and tragically they died soon after. He stayed with his supporter, Colonel Hender Molesworth, as the Governor's residence at Spanish Town was in a state of disrepair. Morgan had never used it, preferring to do his business in Port Royal, and resided at his handsome new plantation house at Llanrumney. On the day of his arrival, May 14th, Lynch gave Sir Harry a letter cancelling his commission as both Lieutenant-Governor and Lieutenant-General of Jamaica. Morgan was ordered to make a full report on the provisions and fortifications for the defence of the island, and dismissed from power.

No reason was given for Morgan's dismissal and Morgan was astounded and perturbed. He fell once more into heavy drinking, and his health rapidly deteriorated. Like Vaughan, Lynch also complained of Morgan's dissolute behaviour, but the only witness who could be later called against him was a female tavern-keeper who said she heard him say, as Morgan passed her door, *'God damn the Assembly.'* Morgan now spent much of his time with his Tory friends, fellow-councillors Archbold, Byndloss, Ballard, Watson and Elletson in the Loyal Club. Lynch complained: *'In his debauches which go on every night, he is much magnified and little criticised by the five or six little sycophants that share them ... In his drink Sir Henry reflects on the government, swears, damns and curses most extravagantly.'*

In the Assembly, Samuel Long led the largest group, followed by Lynch and Molesworth, and then Morgan's allies. One of Lynch's conditions for returning to Jamaica was that he could suspend any member of the

Council and remove their right to public office. Lynch now had total power.

1682 – 1683

In January, Roger Elletson, who had been Morgan's Attorney General until dismissed by Lynch, spoke out against Protestant dissenters against King Charles. He was one of Morgan's Loyal Club, a supporter of the King, and the Council of Jamaica declared that his speech was malicious. Lynch reported to London that his actions were inspired by Sir Henry Morgan, and bound him over.

While the row between Morgan's dwindling band of supporters and those of Lynch festered, piracy was becoming endemic again. The *Trompeuse* alone captured around 18 British ships off Hispaniola, causing around £50,000 of losses. Morgan stayed out of the arguments, usually at Llanrumney, and only came to Port Royal for prodigious drinking sessions with his supporters. Unfortunately, he was being blackened by his association with Elletson and his nephew Charles Morgan, both of whom were increasingly vociferous in their criticism of Lynch.

On October 10, Byndloss was removed from the Council for disorderly conduct. He was dismissed from public office and membership of the militia. On the 11th, it was the turn of Henry's cousin and brother-in-law Charles Morgan, son of Edward, who was stripped of his commission as Commandant of Port Royal. On October 12, with no supporters left in the Council, Morgan was also thrown off the Council on a variety of charges. The Council voted Henry to be stripped of '*all his offices and commands and suspended (from) the Council.*'

Sir Hans Sloane, who later accompanied Lord Albemarle to Jamaica, thought that by this time Morgan had liver problems (caused by decades of neat rum), *dropsy* (oedema, or swellings) and chronic pulmonary '*phthisis*' (tuberculosis, possibly caused by his journey under arrest to England years earlier). Henry had organised a party of people around him as Tories, the loyalist party of Charles Stuart, while trying to parade Lynch as a royalty-hating Whig. However, Morgan's influence was waning with his health, and he kept as far away from the hated Lynch as possible.

Footnote:

1. The *Jamaica Merchant* has been seemingly recently salvaged near the 4800-hectare Ile des Vaches (Cow Island). It lies in 10m of water near the site where Morgan's *Oxford* exploded. The diving team of the *Sea Explorer AG*, under the leadership of Klaus Keppler, were looking for the nearby wreck of Morgan's *Oxford*. Morgan had saved or salvaged all the large cannon, (which are probably those now in Fort Charles at Port Royal), but the divers found 8 small cannon, coins, an anchor and a jug dated between 1650 and 1680.

In the Jamaica Government's accounts of the time, there is an entry of a payment to Sir Henry Morgan for *'mounting Great Guns… £7 – 10 shillings'*. On Ile des Vaches, off the south coast of modern Haiti, a new holiday development has been named Port Morgan.

Samuel Pepys, Secretary to the Navy

CHAPTER IX

1684

Lynch had engineered a council full of his supporters. The Governor had previously organised the dismissal of the Welshman Cradock from the Council. Another Morgan supporter, Roger Elletson had been moved off the Council, and he was now even forbidden to practise law. Lynch was in total command of Jamaica. In a last throw of the dice, Henry now sent Charles Morgan to England to protest about Lynch. Lynch now received news that the Lords of Trade had supported him in his actions, and died soon after, on August 24, 1684. Hender Molesworth, a close friend of Vaughan and Lynch, took over as Acting Governor. Life in Jamaica had soured for Sir Harry. He was ill, out of power, and back at London, there were even more problems.

1684 THE FIRST SUCCESSFUL LIBEL SUIT IN HISTORY

Johan Esquemeling, the Fleming who sailed under Morgan, wrote '*De Americaensche Zee Roovers*' in 1678. It was translated into Spanish and French and ran through many editions. Its immense success attracted two English booksellers, Thomas Malthus and William Crooke, who both published translations of the Spanish edition in 1684. In London, Charles Morgan purchased copies, sent them to Sir Harry, and consulted with a lawyer, as the book claimed that Henry had been an indentured servant, was a pirate and was responsible for atrocities. The book was a best-selling sensation in Holland, France, Spain and England, the major powers of the time, and was subtly re-written to appeal to each country. Morgan read a copy of this *History of the Bucaniers* in Jamaica, and immediately instructed his London lawyer, John Greene, to force the publishers to retract the claims about his past. William Crooke complied immediately, promising to put a favourable insert on Morgan in the second edition. The legal action was dropped, especially as Crookes also issued a grovelling pamphlet, which included:

'*I have been credibly informed by certain gentlemen, who belong unto the acquaintance of Sir Henry, that several things are therein delivered, the which are both falsely reported by John Esquemeling, and wrongfully represented, and consequently are much redounding to the Disreputation and Dishonour of that Worthy Person, Sir Henry Morgan; For the Wounds of whose reputation by*

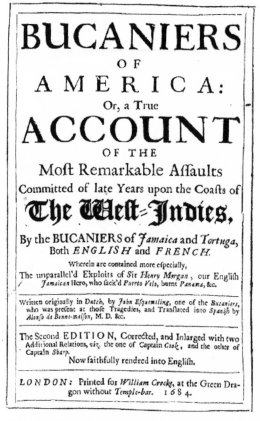

BUCANIERS
OF
A M E R I C A :
Or, a True
ACCOUNT
OF THE
Moſt Remarkable Aſſaults
Committed of late Years upon the Coaſts of

The Weſt-Indies,

By the BUCANIERS of *Jamaica* and *Tortuga*,
Both *ENGLISH* and *FRENCH*.

Wherein are contained more eſpecially,

The unparallel'd Exploits of Sir *Henry Morgan*, our Engliſh
Jamaican Hero, who ſack'd *Puerto Velo*, burnt *Panama*, &c.

Written originally in *Dutch*, by *John Eſquemiling*, one of the *Bucaniers*,
who was preſent at thoſe Tragedies; and Tranſlated into *Spaniſh* by
Alonſo de Bonni-maiſen, M. D. &c.

The Second EDITION, Corrected, and Inlarged with two
Additional Relations, *viz.* the one of Captain *Cook*, and the other of
Captain *Sharp*.
Now faithfully rendred into Engliſh.

LONDON : Printed for *William Crooke*, at the Green Dragon without *Temple-bar.* 1 6 8 4.

that Author, I have been, ever since my better information, both heartily sorrowful, and concerned in the sincerity of my mind; and in testimony thereof, have thought it convenient, by these times, humbly to solicit, and desire the pardon of that noble and generous Spirit, for as much as by me hath been contributed thereunto, by printing the English Translation.'

So far, so good, but Thomas Malthus was unwilling to settle. He seemed to have spread propaganda that Morgan was even more brutal than the book claimed, in order to create more interest and stimulate sales. Morgan and his lawyer seemed to hope the matter would just go away – Morgan could not afford litigation, with his uncertain future. It seems that Morgan did not mind much about the lies told about his behaviour - it was the slur on his pedigree that he cared about. He was spending his time plotting with his supporters in the Loyal Club for his restoration to the island Council. Not one source gave Esquemeling's claims any credibility by supporting them, which is both notable and extraordinary, counting the number of Morgan's enemies in London and Jamaica. An account of Basil Ringrose's raid into the Pacific was now published, with a chapter added on Morgan's attack on Panama, to '*rescue the honour of that incomparable soldier and seaman from the hands of such as would load him with the blackest infamy.*'

Slowly, Morgan's men were being re-elected to the Council. Elletson became the leader of the Tory faction, and Ballard and Archbold joined him. Other friends of Morgan, such as Robert Byndloss also tried to join, and undo the damage carried out by Lynch. It was generally thought that Molesworth was a temporary appointment, and the planters wanted Council control before a new Governor was appointed.

1685

However, in February 1685, the Catholic James II succeeded Charles II as King of England. As he was friendly with Spain, Morgan's alleged past as a murderer and torturer of the Spanish, without proper letters of marque, forced his lawyer to act quickly. The lawyer, John Greene, sought a special hearing by the new king, a '*coram rege*'. He set out to prove Esquemeling was a liar, and that Malthus had disseminated this '*certain false, malicious, scandalous and famous libel entitled 'The History of the Bucaniers*'. Morgan of course was '*of good fame and name, and against evil deeds, piracies and robberies*' and buccaneers were '*thieves*' of which he '*always had and still has hatred*'.

As James had personally profited from Morgan's buccaneering exploits, the new King could not really disapprove this line of attack. Greene then went through the various libels in the book; that Morgan was a bond-servant, a pirate before he privateered under Mansvelt; the Puerto Principe accusations; and various tortures ascribed to Morgan. The lies were so great that the honest and loyal subject might even be tried and hung for piracy! The lawyer concluded his speech by asking for ten thousand pounds damages. Malthus was ordered to appear before the king, but refused to attend. Whether he believed that Morgan had a case, or he was '*warned off*' by some of Morgan's friends in London is unknown. King James refused to recommend an amount for damages, so the sheriffs of Middlesex summoned twelve men for jury service, who awarded Sir Henry £200, with £10 costs, on May 27th. The action was reported in the London Gazette upon June 8th, and the principle that money could be awarded for literary libel had been made a legal precedent.

Malthus' apology was accompanied by the following verse:

> Let the great Morgan, our fam'd Bucanier,
> In his late Enterprise make this appear,
> Who with a handful of brave Englishmen,
> Frighted the whole America of Spain
> And when he was on the Indian shore,
> Had he from England's King derived his power,
> Charles had been crowned the Indies' Emperour.
> Though the Pole brag of their last year's campaign,
> And the French King boast of what he's done to Spain,
> Great Morgan's fame shall last as long as there
> Is beat of Drum or any sound of War.

Also in June, the Duke of Monmouth's rebellion was smashed at Sedgemoor. Christopher Monck, Duke of Albemarle (like Monmouth, a former drinking partner of Morgan's) fought for the king, and wanted the Governorship of Jamaica. Like Morgan, Albemarle desperately needed money – he had gambled, whored, drunk and frittered away most of his father's fortune. The Duke firmly believed that there was a Spanish treasure ship that could be salvaged, off northeast Hispaniola. The ship had foundered in 1659, and both Spanish and French expeditions had tried to find it. King Charles had loaned Albemarle a frigate and ninety-five men in 1682, but he had been unable to locate it. In 1685, a seaman had found some silver ingots, and one of gold, on the shores of Samana Bay, and James promised that Albemarle could try again.

1686

In March, an expedition sailed for the West Indies, mainly financed by Albemarle's depleted resources, and in May it was announced that he would be the new Governor of Jamaica. Morgan was overjoyed – this was a man he could work with. He had no friendship with Governor Molesworth, who was only really interested in working the Asiento slave treaty to his advantage. Molesworth was a factor of the Royal Africa Company, which now had a monopoly on the slave trade with Spain. He had no need for Morgan or any other local leaders – he was too busy making money. Albemarle immediately called for Morgan and Byndloss to be reappointed to the Jamaica Council, but King James vetoed the proposal.

Christopher Monck, 2nd Duke of Albemarle

1687

Early this year, Robert Byndloss, after a run-in with the Admiralty Court, died, and Harry Morgan began looking after the affairs of his old friend's wife (his cousin) and their eight children.

Albemarle was waiting in England, waiting anxiously for the return of his two ships. Morgan desperately wanted him to come out to Jamaica, to restore him to the Council. In June 1687, the ships returned, carrying loot salvaged from the galleon to the value of a third of a million pounds. They could not carry any more bullion and had to return for more later. The newly rich

Duke of Albemarle sent more ships out to salvage, and sailed to Jamaica for three days of roistering with Sir Henry. He arrived on December 20th. Morgan now assumed his rightful position as (unofficial) chief advisor to the Governor. Albemarle again proposed that Morgan join the Council of Jamaica, but King James prevaricated, saying that Morgan would have to return to England and plead his case. Morgan was ill, and feared that such a trip would kill him. Albemarle made yet another plea after lobbying Council support: 'One thing I have omitted to mention to your Lordships, as you will find by the minutes of the Council concerning Sir Henry Morgan, where the whole Council have desired me that I would favourable recommend him to your Majestie for re-admission into the Council which I earnestly do, and desire your Lordships will please to move it to his Majestie.'

1688

In July, Albemarle and Morgan received news from Whitehall that Morgan was back on the Council. Morgan carried on drinking heavily, and frequented the lowest places in Port Royal. Dr Hans Sloane[1] had sailed with the Duke and Duchess of Albemarle in order to look after the 27-year-old duchess, who was showing sings of mental instability, possibly brought on by her husband's frittering away of her immense fortune. The 34-year-old Duke was also in poor health, possibly brought on by alcoholism.

Albemarle told Morgan that the Lords of Trade were still unwilling for him to join the Council, but assured him that it would be only a matter of time. Sir Harry at this time, with his legs and stomach swollen, was spending more and more time in his hammock, drinking rum to forget the pain and get to sleep. He was just 53 years old, and far from the fit and swaggering figure that Albemarle remembered from their drinking sessions in London, 14 years previously. Sloane gives us the account of Morgan's last days: *Sir Henry Morgan, aged about 45 (actually 53), lean, sallow coloured, his eyes a little yellowish and his belly jutting out or prominent, complained to me of want of appetite to victuals; he had a kicking or reaching to vomit every morning and generally a small looseness attending him, and withal was much given to drinking and sitting up late, which I supposed had been the cause of his present indisposition.'* After a temporary recovery, *'falling into the old course of life, and not taking any advice to the contrary, his belly swelled so as not to be contained in his coat, on which I warned him of his very great danger because he being so very weak and subject to looseness, there was no room for purging, medicines, which seems to be the greatest remedy for his dropsy, threatening his life.'* Frightened by this prognosis, Morgan called for the attentions of a Negro medicine man, who gave him enemas of urine and *'plastered him all over with clay and water, and by it augmented his cough.'* Sloane's treatment was little better, telling Morgan to eat juniper berries and rub with scorpion oil.

Knowing that he had little time to live, Henry made his will in June, leaving most of his estates across Jamaica to his *'entirely beloved wife Dame Mary Elizabeth Morgan.'* After her death, the estates would pass to Charles Byndloss, the son of Morgan's late brother-in-law Robert, on condition that he and his heirs would take the name of Morgan. If Charles had no male heirs, the estates would pass on to the male heir of his other brother-in-law Henry Archbold, again upon condition of assuming the name of Morgan. The Penkarne Estate was bequeathed to his nephew Morgan Byndloss, when he reached the age of 21. Young Richard Elletson, the son of Morgan's friend and supporter Roger, was given a plantation named Arthur's Land. He left his sister Catherine Lloyd £60 a year, paid via his cousin Thomas Morgan of Tredegar. Roger Elletson had his choice of Morgan's horses, with his blue saddle and a case of silver-tipped pistols. Colonel Thomas Ballard received his green saddle and trappings. Morgan's nephew Thomas Byndloss, and his godsons Henry Archbold and Richard Elletson were all given silver-hilted swords and mourning rings, and Thomas also was given a case of silver-tipped pistols. Mourning rings were also made for his sisters-in-law, his servants, Sir Francis and Lady Watson, Major John Peake, Dr John Longworth and the Duke and Duchess of Albemarle. The trustees were Colonel Ballard, Henry Archbold, Roger Elletson and Charles Byndloss.

In July, a ship arrived from London with the news that Morgan could be reinstated on the Council, and Albemarle quickly called a meeting for the 12th of the month, where Sir Harry was officially restored to favour, with much pomp and ceremony. A new Assembly was voted for, and Morgan and his Tory supporters were all returned, becoming the largest party. Sir Harry was now satisfied – he could die happily – back at the centre of Jamaican affairs. The Assembly met on July 20th, and voted Roger Elletson as Speaker. In his dying days, Morgan had triumphed. Elletson's first act was to deliver a tribute to Morgan, to a packed Assembly, going back over his contributions to the island's survival and independence. Lynch and Molesworth were severely criticised, and Morgan returned to his plantation to die on August 25th 1688 at his Llanrumney estate in Jamaica.

Albemarle gave his great friend a state funeral, with a horse-drawn cortege, and many on foot walking alongside *'having black ribbands, being very seemly dressed in black.'* As noted, the bulk of the property was left to his wife (and cousin) Elizabeth, who lived another 12 years. Certain monies were also put aside for his cousin Thomas Morgan of Tredegar, and for his faithful Welsh servant Evan Davis.

Intriguingly, the Glamorgan historian G.T. Clarke believed that Morgan died in a Spanish prison in 1681. Leslie (1739), Gardner (1839) and Bancroft (1883) all stated that he died in a London prison, the latter *'for he was a ruffian whose hell-born depravity of heart was relieved by no gleam of a better nature.'* Howard Pyle (1897) had Morgan dying in the Tower of London *'for the very deeds for which he was knighted,'* and in *'Raveneau de Lussan'* (1930), Morgan is killed by Caribbean Indians. It is little wonder that Morgan is not renowned as a famous and honourable man.

Henry Morgan's will was eventually signed and sealed at Port Royal on February 19th, 1689:

Sir Henry Morgan late of this Island, Knight, decided as they shall be shown unto them by Dame Mary Elizabeth Morgan his Relief and Executrix thereof, the said Nathaniel Toww and Robert Goodler offices of them are to make a true return unto our Governor of our said Island unto their own offices of their hands and seals together with this present power annered1 so that the said inventory and appraisement may be recorded in the Secretary's office or this our island – witness Sir Francis Watson Knight President of the Council and Governor of our said Island of Jamaica and the territories thereon depending and Counsellor of the same the Thirtieth day of October 1688.

(Signed) Hickam, Secretary and Francis Watson

According to the power to me by the within written writ given I did on the within named Peter Heywood and John Moone Esps administrator of the oath to them that by the said writ is dis(pensed?) witness my hand and shall this Eleventh day of February in the fifth year of his Majesty's reign.

Robert Heedler

An Inventory and Appraisement of the Gods and Chattels, Rights and Credits of the Honourable Sir Henry Morgan Knight as shown unto us this 19th February 1689.

	£ - s – d
Wrought (silver) plate – 196 pounds at 5 shillings 2 pence a pound	128.02.08
One silver watch	3.00.00
Two gold rings with ord. stones	2.00.00
Two plain gold rings	10.00
Two pair white buttons and 3 pair shoe buckles	5.00
A set of gold buckles and buttons set with (precious) stones	4.10.00
Some emerald drops and a lump of pomander²	7.00
One ounce of small p ashe (?)	1.00.00
One ounce and 18 (dram?) wrought gold	7.10.00
Nine small Coker nutts (coconuts) tipped with silver	9.00
A parcel³ of glasses	1.10.00
A parcel of china tea cups and earthenware	1.10.00
A parcel of agate hafted and other old knives	1.00.00
Two brass horizontal dials and a small compass	10.00
Three dozen woven chain (rattan) chairs	10.00.00
Sixteen old chairs	1.00.00
A parcel old tables	6.00.00
One silk mohair suite of curtains lined with Persian with bed, coverlid etc.	30.00.00
Four feather beds with bolsters	30.00.00
Fourteen hamakoes (hammocks)	14.00.00
A musketo (mosquito) net	1.00.00
One flock bed etc.	10.00
Six purple bays (baize?) gowns	3.00.00
Five looking glasses	5.00.00
Two inlaid scriptores (writing desks)	20.00.00
One plain scriptore	1.00.00
One inlaid chest of drawers, table, stand etc.	10.00.00
One cedar chest of drawers	2.00.00
One dressing box cabinet etc.	2.10.10
123 bound books	50.00.00
A parcel of old charts, maps etc.	5.00.00
A parcel of sermons, plays and pamphlets	1.00.00
A parcel of sheets and pillow boors(?)	28.00.00
A parcel of Diaper Table cloths and napkins	12.00.00
A parcel of damask ditto	5.00.00
A parcel of Ozenbrigg⁴ napkins	3.00.00
A parcel of damask diapers and Ozenbrigg towels	1.10.10
Six side board cloths	1.00.00
Six old cushions	6.00
Three remnants of Holland⁵ (cloth)	10.10.03
Several remnants of coarse linen	2.00.00
Three and a half yards of Cambric (linen)	10.00
Sir Henry's wearing linen (clothes?)	50.00.00

	£ - s – d
Two silk night gowns	9.00.00
Three old beaver hats	5.00.00
Two pair of laced gloves	1.00.00
A barber's and tweezers cases and instruments	1.05.00
Two prospect glasses[6] and other old things	3.00.00
A parcel of chests, trunks and a press	5.00.00
A velvet saddle etc.	2.01.00
A waist belt	5.00
27 guns and 19 cartoush (cartridge) boxes	55.00.00
Three pair pistols and three swords	16.00.00
Five powder horns and two lances	1.00.00
Nine pictures	35.00.00
A clock	10.00.00
Four sconces	1.10.00
A pair of old tables with a box of troy weights	1.00.00
Three close stools and pans[7]	2.10.00
One cold still (for brewing/fermenting)	2.00.00
A pair of andirons[8]	1.10.03
A jack, 5 iron pots, 5 spits, 2 frying pans & cook room utensils	15.00.00
A parcel of tin ware	2.10.00
5 brass kettles and other brass and copper ware belonging to the cook room	30.00.00
36 ounces of pewter	10.05.00
A parcel of beeswax	2.00.00
A pair of stillyards[9]	1.10.00
25 pounds of candles	12.06
A parcel of soap	2.10.00
A parcel of spices	11.03
A parcel of fruit	2.01.09
Half a barrel of flour	3.10.00
A Dantswirk[10] case of bottles with a parcel of bottles and jars	10.00
A Cassadar[11] iron	10.00
A casting net	10.00
A parcel of baskets and brushes	10.00
A parcel of wooden ware	1.10.00
Three dozen and 3 pair shoes	11.14.00
Eleven barrels of beef[12]	13.15.00
A parcel of salt 1.	10.00
A parcel of old carpenters' tools	10.00
44 Negro men at £20	880.00.00
42 Negro women at £17	165.00.00
13 Negro boys at £8	104.00.00
20 Negro girls at £7	140.00.00
2 Indians at £17	34.00.00
11 white (indentured) servants (with) from one to seven years to serve (their bond)	88.00.00
35 working steers at £7	252.00.00
4 bulls and 4 bulkings[13]	28.00.00

	£ - s – d
21 cows and 6 yearlings	93.00.00
5 heifers	15.00.00
20 mules	240.00.00
8 horses	64.00.00
A mare filly and a horse colt	8.00.00
A parcel of hogs	35.00.00
A parcel of goats	12.00.00
A parcel of dunghill fowls, turkeys, 5 ducks and geese	20.00.00
A gang of dogg (a pack of hounds?)	5.00.00
65,000 weight of muscovado sugar at 2s6d (2 shillings 6 pence) per £ (for rum-making)	406.05.00
640 gallons of rum	26.13.04
1000 gallons molasses	12.10.00
1000 wooden pots	75.00.00
2 rum butts, 2 pipes and 2 iron-bound puncheons[14]	2.00.00
2 mills, 6 with cases, gudgeon[15] stops etc.	120.00.00
2 spare gudgeons	5.00.00
6 spare brasses	10.00.00
8 capooses[16] and 6 stops	4.00.00
2 iron crows (crowbars) and 6 splitting wedges (for making barrels)	1.00.00
6 copper string	65.00.00
1 new copper (still)	23.00.06
4 ladles and 8 skimmers	3.10.00
2 potting basons	2.10.00
6 lamps and 2 scrapers	5.00
A receiver and 6 wooden coolers	2.00.00
3 stills, worms(distilling pipes) and tubs hung	50.00.00
8 dripps[17]	4.00
6 barricoes[18]	10.00
A parcel of nails	5.00
A parcel of plantation tools	15.00.00
8 yokes fixed with chains	5.00.00
A pair of steadd (studded?) wheels	8.00.00
A pair of plain wheels	4.00.00
A hempen rope and 2 single blocks	2.10.00
4 old coppers	12.00.00
A parcel of old copper, old iron tools and several other old things about the house and Sir Henry's Plantation	3.00.00
A parcel of horses and mares running at Coleburry and Ivys savannas	25.00.00
DEBTS due TO the Estate are:	
Imp from Col. George Woodham a bond of £300	150.00.00
From the executor of his Grace the Duke of Albemarle	344.12.00
From Mr Thomas Pinatbrase	35.00.00
From Sir Richard Doreham	60.16.00
From Mr Thomas Byndleys (Byndloss)	290.00.00

£5263.01.03

Signed: Peter Heywood, John Moone

Footnotes:

1. *Annered – the origin of this word is unknown.*
2. *A pomander was a lump of perfume carried about one's person, usually in the form of a ball, to hide odours. It came to refer later to a box, which contained such perfume, usually on the end of a chain, carried or worn by ladies.*
3. *A parcell (sic) meant a quantity of something.*
4. *Oznabrig was a rough German cloth.*
5. *Holland, or Holland cloth, was the name for the strongest linen. The flax from the Netherlands and Flanders was so excellent for producing linen fabric, that the strongest cloth until the 18th century was known as Holland.*
6. *Prospect glasses were popular miniature telescopes, which later became the small binoculars used as opera glasses.*
7. *Portable toilets, lavatories.*
8. *An andiron was an iron for holding logs in a fireplace.*
9. *A stillyard, or stellyard, was used for clearing land. It was a type of pickaxe, with a flat adze-shaped blade at either end, which could dig up and slice through tree roots.*
10. *Dantswirk – origin unknown.*
11. *Cassadar iron – origin unknown.*
12. *Beef could not be kept in a hot climate, so was salted and kept in barrels.*
13. *A bulking may be a heifer.*
14. *Butts are large casks, each capable of holding 2 hogsheads or rum. Pipes are similar tubs, holding the same quantity, about 126 gallons. Puncheons are, in this context, casks that variously hold 84 or 120 gallons.*
15. *A gudgeon is a pin of iron fastened in the end of a wooden shaft or axle, in which it turns.*
16. *Capoose – unknown origin.*
17. *Dripp – unknown, but possibly a piece of distilling equipment.*
18. *Barricoes are kegs, usually holding water, but probably for rum in the context.*

Governor Albemarle ordered a state funeral, with a salute of 22 guns, but died himself of jaundice and dropsy upon October 6th. 'The Sword of England', 'The Admiral of the Brethren of the Coast', 'Good Old Sir Harry' was buried in Port Royal. In August 1688, Captain Lawrence Wright of HMS Assistance noted the occasion: 'Saturday 25. This day about 11 hours noon Sir Henry Morgan died, & the 26th was brought over from Passage-fort to the King's house at Port Royal, from thence to the Church, & after a sermon was carried to the Pallisadoes and there buried. All the forts fired an equal number of guns, we fired two & twenty and after we & the Drake had fired, all the merchant men fired.' A few years later the historian Leslie noted 'he showed the world that he was qualified to govern as well as fight, and that in all stations of life, he was a great man.' Henry had been Jamaica's Lieutenant-Governor and major protector on three occasions, in 1675, 1678 and 1680.

The historian Edward Long wrote in 1774 that Sir Henry 'whose achievements are well known, was equal to any of the most renowned warriors of historical fame, in valour, conduct and success, but this gentleman has been unhappily confounded with the piratical herd.' Twenty years later, another

Jamaican planter, Bryan Edwards, criticised Esquemeling's treatment of Morgan, saying that 'By the kindness of a friend in this island I have had the opportunity of perusing some of Sir Henry Morgan's original private letters; and this I will say, that they manifest such a spirit of humanity, justice, liberality, and piety, as prove he has either been grossly traduced or that he was the greatest hypocrite living - a character ill-suited to the frank and fearless temper of the man.' He also noted that the English translation of Esquemeling was not taken from the Dutch original, but from the Spanish translation, thereby further skewing opinion against Morgan. Sir Harry had an amazing and courageous life, but is virtually ignored in English history. One has to ask why. He joins a roster of Welsh heroes such as Owain Glyndwr and Owain Llawgoch who are virtually unknown Britons, probably because of the over-emphasis upon England at all levels of education.

In 1690, just two years after Morgan's death, Sir Dalby Thomas wrote 'An Historical Account of the Rise and Growth of the West India Colonies and of the Great Advantages they are to England, in respect to Trade', in which he eulogised Sir Harry thus: Sir Henry Morgan commonly called Panama Morgan, for his Glorious undertaking and conquest of the Spaniard of that place... took and ransacked a Town (Panama)... This Man as great an honour to our Nation and terror to the Spanish as ever were born in it... he had done nothing but by Commission of the Governor and Council of Jamaica... was upon a Letter from the Secretary of State sent into England a Prisoner, and without being charged with any Crime, or even brought to a Hearing, he was kept here at his own great Expense above Three year.'

As the Reverend J. Leoline Phillips stated, in his speech to the Glamorgan Society in London, in 1910: 'As a leader of men it is a question whether Morgan has ever been surpassed: this is proved by the success of his march to Panama in the face of stupendous difficulties. Brave himself, he seemed to have the capacity to inspire his followers with daring. His escape from Maracaybo (sic) and his many other well-planned schemes of offence and defence show him to have been a tactician and strategist of the highest order. He left a name at which any rate the Spanish seaboard grew pale, and we men of Glamorgan can quote him with confidence as a hero whose exploits equalled those of the spacious times of Elizabeth.'

Brigadier-General E.A. Cruickshank, in his 'The Life of Sir Henry Morgan' (1935, Macmillan Canada) fittingly ends his book thus: 'His talents as an organiser and administrator of a considerable fleet manned by volunteers, and his conduct as a leader of such a turbulent force in very daring undertakings were most remarkable. Skill in preparation and planning were combined with decision and dauntless courage in their execution. Francis Drake *had not ventured to attack Puerto Bello. The formidable force sent out by Admiral Vernon seventy years later, having taken that place, declined to attempt crossing the isthmus for the capture of Panama. Morgan's outstanding ability as a commander is beyond dispute.'*

> You was a wise one, Morgan
> You was a knowing knave
> When you was in your cabin
> But now you're in your grave!
>
> You was a flyer, Morgan
> You was the lad to crowd,
> When you was in your flagship
> But now you're in your shroud
>
> You was a stayer, Morgan
> You was the lad to go
> Across the starving Isthmus,
> But now you've gone below
>
> You was a great one, Morgan
> You was a king uncrowned,
> When you was under canvas
> But now you're in your shroud
> You was a great one, Morgan
> The greatest of them all
> You'll ne'er go back to Wales
> Port Royal saw your fall

- (old Jamaican song, with the last verse added by the author)

THE DESTRUCTION OF PORT ROYAL

In the late 17th century, Port Royal and Boston vied for the title of the largest English town in the Americas. That was the measure of its importance. Between 1655 and 1692 it was the fastest growing of all the towns founded by the English in the Americas, and was easily the most economically important English port there. Of its 6,500-7,000 inhabitants, around half were involved in privateering. (Boston had a population of 6000 in 1690). There were 2000 buildings, some of 4 storeys and built with brick. In 1685, 313 ships visited, compared to 226 in all the ports of New England. It was the mercantile centre of the

The defences Morgan built at Fort Charles, Port Royal

Caribbean, with coins being used for currency, unlike the commodity exchange of the other English colonies.

Port Royal lay on a small cay at the tip of the long sand spit called the Palisadoes, which forms Kingston Harbour. On June 7th, 1692, a combined earthquake and tidal wave destroyed two-thirds of this buccaneer capital, sweeping Captain Morgan's grave into the sea. The tremors had rocked the sandy peninsula on which Port Royal was built, and caused buildings to slide and slip into the sea. Apart from the 2000 that died on that day, another 3000 died later from wounds, disease and fever. In the tidal wave that followed the earthquake, *'nothing else was seen but the dead and dying, and heard but shrieks and cries.'* So few people were left alive that the bodies just floated in and out with the tide, and rolled along the beaches. A joiner, John Pike, wrote to his brother and told him that his house was lost beneath the waves: *'I lost my wife, my son, an apprentice, a white-maid and 6 slaves and all that I ever had in the world. My land where I was ready to raise 5 houses, and had room to raise 10 more, is all sunk, a good sloop may sail over it as well as over the Point.'*

The capital of St Jago de la Vega, corrupted to Santiago, now resumed its authority over Jamaica's affairs. Port Royal was partially rebuilt after the earthquake, only to suffer a great fire in 1703. In 1712 Governor Hamilton reported that a hurricane had destroyed 38 ships at Port Royal and 9 at Kingston. Storms, hurricanes and two more earthquakes in 1722 and 1744 meant that the town was reduced to a British naval station with a dockyard, which closed in 1905. Chaloner Ogle was anchored on *HMS Swallow*, off Port Royal on August 28th, 1722, and reported '*there was as much wind in my opinion as could possibly blow out of the heavens ... all the merchantmen in the harbour foundered or drove ashore excepting one sloop.*' It is the only sunken town in the New World, and efforts are being made to have it declared a World Heritage Site, '*an underwater Pompeii*'. Underwater excavation has enabled us to 'rewalk' the narrow streets of Port Royal today, and perhaps even Henry Morgan's grave may be found. Texas A&M University's Nautical Archaeology Programme has reconstructed the life of the town's main pewterer, Simon Benning, from the silver cutlery and many stamped pewter plates found on the site. Excavations centred for 10 years on the submerged 17th century remains of Lime Street, near its intersection with Queen Street and High Street, in Port Royal's commercial centre. Eight buildings have been excavated.

The riddle of what happened to Morgan's '*treasure*' has never been resolved. It was believed that he had concealed it somewhere between Panama and Jamaica, or perhaps a substantial portion went to King Charles. In the mid-1960's, the American marine archaeologist Robert

Marx, working for the Jamaican government, found a treasure chest at Port Royal. The wooden chest crumbled almost immediately, leaving only a brass lock, so no identification was made of its owner, except that the chest bore the crest of the Spanish king. It was filled with hundreds of silver coins, most minted at the silver centres of Potosi in Colombia, and Lima in Peru. They dated from Morgan's raid. Could there be more of Morgan's treasure to find at Port Royal? Or is there more loot on the Ile des Vaches?

If you go today to Port Royal, on a 20-minute ferry ride from Kingston's West Dock, all that is left is a small fishing village of 2000 people. Alternatively drive out along the Palisadoes, the long narrow spit of land leading out from Kingston. Only Fort Charles (formerly Fort Cromwell) survives intact of the six forts of Harry Morgan's time, and is the oldest surviving structure in Port Royal, along with the remains of Fort Rupert. The young Horatio Nelson was stationed here in 1779. The silver communion plate in St Peter's Church is supposed to have been given by Morgan, looted from Panama. (St Peters's was built in 1725, to replace Christ Church, which was lost in 1692). You can stay at Morgan's Harbour Hotel and Beach Club, which includes the largest marina in Kingston, and eat at Sir Henry Morgan's Restaurant, overlooking Kingston Bay. A Jamaica National Heritage Trust plaque in the old Muster Grounds reads: *Once called "the richest and wickedest city in the world", Port Royal was also the virtual capital of Jamaica. To it came men of all races, treasures of silks, doubloons and gold from Spanish ships, looted on the high seas by the notorious 'Brethren of the Coast' as the pirates were called. From here sailed the fleets of Henry Morgan, later lieutenant-governor of Jamaica, for the sacking of Camaguey, Maracaibo, and Panama, who died here, despite the ministrations of his Jamaican folk-doctor. Admirals Lord Nelson and Benbow, and the chilling Edward 'Blackbeard' Teach were among its inhabitants. The town flourished for 32 years until at 20 minutes to noon, June 7, 1692. It was partially buried in the sea by an earthquake.*

Footnote:
1. Hans Sloane was made a Fellow of the Royal College of Physicians on the 12th April 1687. He sailed for the West Indies on the frigate *Assistance* on the 12th September in his capacity as physician to the Duke of Albermarle. The ship reached Madeira on the 21st October and left on the 23rd after taking on board provisions. Sloane observed dolphins, flying fish, a grampus (a whale) and, on November 5th, he spied a Tropicbird. The ship reached Barbados on the 25th November and Sloane was allowed ashore to go collecting specimens of plants and other curios. The ship also put into port in St Lucia (6th December) and Dominica (7th December) before reaching Jamaica on the 19th December. Sloane was immediately called upon to act as physician to the ailing Sir Henry

Morgan. Sloane observed wildlife, collected seeds and specimens, and reported to the Royal Society on events such as the earthquake in Lima in 1687. In 1688, the Duke of Albermarle died. Sloane had built a collection of plants native to the West Indies and made notes for his work in this area. Sloane received news of the Glorious Revolution in England and of William III arriving in London on the 19th December. James II fled to France and William III and Mary were crowned. In 1689, Hans Sloan accompanied the deranged Duchess of Albermarle on the return voyage to England, with the embalmed body of her husband (his bowels were buried in Spanish Town). When they arrived home in May they were unsure as to who was king. Sloane brought back c.800 plant specimens. He later converted his home in Great Russell Street, London, into a wonderful museum, which is still in existence today.

Addendum

Typical of the calumnies that Morgan suffered to harm his reputation is a book supposedly written in the 17th century, by Robert Williams. His *Memoirs of a Buccaneer* was first published in 1990 by Rio Grand Press of New Mexico. It is a potboiler, making the case for the fictional Captain Pemberthy of the West Country to be head of the Brethren of the Coast. It is doubtful whether Williams ever saw the West Indies, and most of the account seems to be based upon Esquemeling's book. He says that the brethren '*had already chosen as their leader Captain Morgan, a self-seeking, libidinous goat of a Welshman, with a smooth tongue and devil's heart, who had lately had some success among the Spaniards on the Isle of Cuba, where he had sacked Puerto Principe.*'

Williams hated Morgan for serving '*a lewd Scotch king* (Charles II) *(who) was brought back from penury and the slums and stews (brothels) of Europe to reign over us, whose death alone relieved England of his iniquities.*' Captain Pemberthy had told Morgan '*plainly that is was impossible for decent, self-respecting Englishmen to serve under such a Welsh miscreant*', for '*a more treacherous villain I dare vouch the reader has never known.*' He railed against '*that accursed Welshman, who then and afterwards brought such great dishonour on the English name, and was knighted therefore by our Scotch king*'.

However, there is one interesting part of the book that refers to '*the terrible march from Chagres across the Isthmus, where they all grew light-headed for days together from the effects of hunger and fatigue.*' It is a song:

> To the Port of Panama,
> The Spaniards from afar
> Bring the treasure of their empire overseas;
> Costly cargoes o'er the deep
> Till the gold there grows as cheap,
> Ay, cheaper than the pence with you and me.
>
> There are soft and pleasant airs
> At Panama;
> The tempest ever spares
> Panama;
> With their wines no wine compares;
> No tobacco is like theirs:
> 'Tis the same with all their wares
> At Panama.

'Tis a city fair and great,
Panama.
The Spaniards lives in state
At Panama:
Comely women on him wait,
Every whim of his to sate;
Every warehouse teems with plate
At Panama.

But the Inquisition reigns
At Panama,
And the priesthood ever strains
At Panama;
With the rack and with the stake,
To make man the truth forsake,
And freedom's heart to break
At Panama.

'Tis Belshazzar's feast today,
And the women all are gay
As they dance before their master in the hall.
In the balance thou art weighed:
Nor will vengeance now bestayed.
See the writing; read the writing on the wall.

Panama, Panama,
Thy course is well-nigh run;
Thou shalt be as Babylon,
As the cities of the dead that are gone.
Panama, Panama,
Babylon.

PARTIAL BIBLIOGRAPHY

H.R. Allen – Buccaneer Admiral Henry Morgan 1951

Philip Ayres – The Voyages and Adventures of Capt. Barth. Sharp and others in the South Sea... Morgan his Expedition against the West Indies... 1684

C.H. Baring – The Buccaneers of the West Indies in the 17th Century - 1910

Clinton V. Black – Our Archives 1962

Richard Blome – A Description of the Island of Jamaica 1672

T.D. Breverton – The Book of Welsh Pirates and Buccaneers 2003

Calendar of State Papers: Colonial Series (various)

E.A. Cruickshank – The Life of Sir Henry Morgan 1935

Peter Earle – The Sack of Panama 1981

A.O. Esquemeling – The Buccaneers of America 1684, reprinted 1969, trans. Alexis Brown

Peter R. Galvin – Patterns of Pillage – A Geography of Caribbean-based Piracy in Spanish America

Charles Leslie – New History of Jamaica 1740

Philip Lindsay – The Great Buccaneer 1976

Sandra Maria Petrovich – Henry Morgan's Raid on Panama – Geopolitics and Colonial Ramifications 2001

Dudley Pope – Harry Morgan's Way 1977

W. Adolphe Roberts – Sir Henry Morgan: Buccaneer and Governor 1952

Robert Williams – Memoirs of a Buccaneer, 1990 reprint

A. Winston – No Purchase, No Pay 1969